Democracy—The Old and the New.

SPEECH

OF

HON. JOHN HICKMAN, OF PENN.,

ON THE BATTLE GROUND OF BRANDYWINE,

SEPTEMBER 11, 1860.

Mr. HICKMAN said:

FELLOW CITIZENS, LADIES, AND GENTLEMEN: In my remarks, at this time, I shall have but little to say about men. I prefer to speak of that with which I am more intimately acquainted. My subject, to-day, is Democracy—the old and the new; or, Democracy as it was, and as it is.

The object of those who achieved our independence of the Government of England was, not so much to be relieved from grievances which then affected them, as to establish defences against the danger of future oppression. Our fathers were not selfish, but philanthropic. They did not regard themselves alone, but posterity. They were patriots in that sense in which the word should be understood. If they had not looked beyond their own day, they would have temporized; they would have done worse—they would have compromised. But fixing their eyes upon a distant age, they contended for an enduring principle. They believed that man—that universal man—had natural rights to be regarded in all human laws, and that they could only be lost sight of under tyranny; that the greatest of these was liberty, and that death even was to be preferred to slavery. I do not say that this made up Democracy, but I do assert that there can be no genuine Democracy without this sentiment.

It is not to be believed that there can be a general Democracy without liberty; and it is next to impossible that there should be liberty without Democracy. Democracy being the power of the people to rule themselves, makes it the most perfect guaranty the masses can have for individual and collective prosperity. Anything short of this, places a people at the mercy of a man or a junto. Under republics, freedom cannot be lost without utter depravity. Under other forms of government, it cannot exist without almost superhuman virtue. Herein lies the value of popular power, and the danger of monarchies and aristocracies.

It was natural that the great leading idea of the Revolution should be embodied in the Declaration of our Independence. And accordingly we there find the enunciation that all men are created equal, and endowed with the inalienable right of liberty; that Governments derive their just powers from the consent of the governed; and that it is the right of a people to alter or abolish old Governments, and to institute new. In a word, the equality of man, and his right to control Government, are made most conspicuous and emphatic. If our ancestors had insisted upon less, they would have failed to relieve themselves of monarchical severity, and their struggles and trials could have resulted in no lasting good.

It is but recently the discovery has been made that the expressive phrase, "all men," is capable of very diverse interpretations, and, like the Cincinnati platform, can be so read as to suit all interests and opinions. At the time of which I speak, slavery, not of the white man merely, but of all races, was felt to be a crime against nature, and it had no advocates as a right. It was reserved for politicians of more doubtful patriotism, if not sagacity, to inform the world that it is theocratic and the highest type of civilization. Herein lies my subject. In the teachings of the fathers, I find the ancient Democracy, and in that of the dissenters the modern.

It was Thomas Jefferson who declared "all men are created equal," and clothed by nature with the right to control Government. That consistent patriot, long reverenced as the father of the Democratic party, proclaimed these sentiments to the world, and at a time, too, when an enunciation of them was fraught with the greatest peril. It was not old John Brown, or William Lloyd Garrison, or Wendell Phillips, haranguing Northern Abolitionists in a peaceful village, but the immortal Jefferson, a son of the South, addressing a people—the nations—when to do so caused him to stake life and fortune and honor. He was founding a Republic, and he promulgated the only truths upon which free government can ever rest. Unless men are created equal, there cannot be equality of rights among the component members of a State, and without the power to control Government there cannot be safeguards for liberty.

But what were the particular opinions of the great American statesman upon the question now so widely distracting us? You will pardon me if I attempt to indicate them in brief. He made no effort to conceal them; on the contrary, he gave to them all possible publicity. He declared slavery to be made up of the most unremitting despotism and degrading submission, leading the child to give way to the worst passions. That the man who could retain his manners and morals under such circumstances was a prodigy. That he who would permit one half of the citizens to trample on the rights of the other half, transforming the one into despots and the other into enemies, should be loaded with execration. That the liberties of the nation could only be secure as long as the conviction remained in the minds of the people that these liberties were the gift of God. That the abolition of slavery even was to him an earnest desire, and that he waited with patience the workings of an overruling Providence to deliver the bondman. These were his judgments, not for a single year merely, or for five or ten years, but throughout a lifetime. And when approaching his death, alluding again to the subject, he writes:

"My sentiments have been forty years before the public; had I repeated them forty times, they would have only become the more stale and threadbare."

Strange and startling expressions to fall from one who claimed to be a Democrat. It is a great pity he does not live in our day, when he could be taught better things. There is not a petty Federal office-holder between Maine and California—not one pitiable partisan in the North, who glories in doing the bidding of his Southern overseer—who would not inform him of his fanaticism and treachery.

Thomas Jefferson, before he framed the Declaration, when he framed the Declaration, after he framed the Declaration; before he was President, whilst he was President, after he was President, thought slavery a curse, both to the white and the black races, and repugnant to every principle of liberty. What Democrat at the present time can say he so believes, and hope to be treated as orthodox in his faith? Your Caleb Cushings, Daniel S. Dickinsons, and General Joseph Lanes, know too well what party fealty requires of them to venture upon such utterances. Even Stephen A. Douglas, wishing to keep one foot within the circle of the Democratic organization, has found it necessary to use all his ingenuity to conceal his thoughts upon the subject. I do but state that which we all must have observed, when I say that all that is required, in this eighty-fifth year of independence, for a freeman to prove that he has no Democracy in him, is his naked avowal that slavery is a vice, and consequently should not be extended. The father of Democracy denounced the institution as criminal, but we, who revere his name, and wish to follow in his footsteps, may not so regard it without the most unmeasured denunciation from our own servants—from an oblique President down to low-priced postmasters.

Democracy, originally, was "hostility to every form of tyranny over the mind of man;" now it is the handmaid of a more galling and debasing slavery than ever before existed in a Christianized nation. In this respect there is no real distinction to be drawn between the two parties professing to sustain Democracy. I take pleasure in making the admission that there are many notable individual exceptions; but still the adherents of Mr. Douglas, as a body, are as willing as those of Mr. Breckinridge to bear witness against the exactions of slavery, although they constantly cry out against its injustice to their chief. I have never doubted, and, assuredly, it is now too late to doubt, that all that is needed to purchase their full support of the broadest demands of the institution, is its promise of a full support of them in return. In the South, all parties defend the relation of master and slave; they even go to the extent of ascribing to it a Divine parentage. What Democrat in the North, trusted to speak, declaims against either its principles or practices? They are not ignorant; they have not read in vain; and they know that it is uncongenial to growth, and advancement, and virtue. They know that for more than half a century the spread of slavery was discouraged and resisted, and that the power of Congress to prevent its extension was admitted both by word and deed. They know that this power is now denied flatly, and that we are to be forced to allow that it has constitutional guaranties upon every foot of our soil outside of State limits. And yet who of them all takes such a position of resistance to these new claims as to make us feel secure in his hands? There is not one. The reason for this is but too apparent. The soul of Democracy, from a spirit of freedom, has become changed into a spirit of slavery. It denies the equality of man. Its sympathies are for the South, and against the North. It has become a synonym of sectionalism. There is a glaring danger threatening our very existence; a deadly serpent coils itself, in open day and before our eyes, around the vitals of the Republic, and Democracy heeds it not. Slavery infuses its poison into the life-blood of the North, paralyzing our powers, and yet Northern Democrats seem to approve the act. Do they not see, do we not all see, that the interests of freedom and slavery conflict, and that Government is wielded for the benefit of the despotism? Is it not recorded against the Democratic party, that they sustained the most flagrant of frauds in Kansas, to crush out rightful rule? That they exhausted artifice to force a slave State into the Union against the wishes of the people, and to exclude free States in defiance of the popular will, and in violation of their own determined legislation? Are these the fruits of the teachings of Jefferson? Can this be the old Democracy? Is it not the new? What shall we say, what do, finding that Presidents pledged to our views, to do right, fearing the South, turn, Arnold-like, to betray us, to work out iniquity? What ought we to say, what do, when Cabinets are so chosen, Senatorial committees selected, and offices everywhere filled, as to subsidize the North for the aggrandizement of the South, to enable them to rule over us forever? The friends of Breckinridge and Douglas alike reply, "Nothing!" "Nothing!" Say nothing! do nothing! Most consistent Democracy this, to elevate Liberty by thrusting Freedom beneath the heavy hob-nailed foot of Slavery! Mr. Breckinridge is the Jupiter Tonans for slavery, and he would not have us get excited on the subject, or his noise might cease to affright us. Mr. Douglas is a political hermaphrodite, a giant of the neuter gender, and he would not advise us to take sides with white labor, lest he should be thought a man, nor with black labor, lest he should be known as a woman. One word! Speak! Act! Let *us*, also, have an eye to terrify, a tongue to threaten, an arm to execute. Why should we not maintain our dignity, our honor, our interests, our people? Is it unlawful? If so, then how great has been the outrage practiced upon us! The time has come for us to take sides, to turn our faces either to the North or the South; those who look upon the ground will be crushed to powder beneath the massy wheels of the chariot bearing the ark of our destiny.

Fellow citizens, another gold-bearing State, of large agricultural capabilities, is about to rise on our western border. Those who are striving to people it are moving from the North and the South toward the Territory. On the one hand you will discover your kinsmen and neighbors, from the farm, the manufactory, and the workshop, carrying with them the institutions of freedom; on the other hand, you will observe the master and his ignorant and vicious bondmen, dragging after them the institution of slavery. The one seek peaceful homes, where by honest industry they may support families and educate free-born children; the other will breed children for the market, and blast the earth into barrenness. These two classes of emigrants will battle for the supremacy, for they cannot live side by side; that is impossible. Have we any sympathy to extend to either? or are we entirely unconcerned as to how the contest may terminate? If we desire the success of the despot whose gang trudges with heavy and broken step, to the clanking of chains and the sobs of the desolate, we will support Mr. Breckinridge. If, however, we have been able to cut ourselves off so far from the impulses of a true humanity as to be unable to choose, or if we have become false enough to decline to choose between the two orders, between right and wrong, we should sustain Douglas; he would be our representative man. But if we have brain and heart and soul enough to appreciate the doctrines of Jefferson and the trials of the poor, if we would bless that community which moves with light and elastic tread to the song of the plowman, the hum of the rapid wheel, and the ring of the anvil, we will distinguish our duty, and do it, regardless of denunciation, knowing that God and all good men will be with us: we will vote for Mr. Lincoln. When the harvest shines in gold, let no one be laggard. When victory is within our reach, let no one quail. When dominion is offered, let it not be surrendered to a foe. I have somewhere read, that when Gaudet was taken by Maria Antoinette into the room where the Dauphin of France was sleeping, he moved aside the curling hair which overshadowed the countenance of the fair boy, and, kissing him, said to the mother, "Educate him for liberty, madame—it is the condition of his life." And I say to you, to all, educate yourselves for liberty; it is the condition of *your* lives. Our fathers fought for freedom, and accomplished it; our fathers valued freedom, and bequeathed it; and, if true to ourselves, like them, we will defend it to the last—*to the last.*

The Democratic party was founded by a wise man upon the leading truths, the indisputable natural rights, to which I have referred, as upon a rock. The foolish have torn it down, and rebuilt it upon the sand, and when the rains shall descend, and the floods come, and the winds blow and beat upon it, and it shall fall, great will be the fall thereof. The only hope for those loitering within its cracked and tottering walls lies in early and swift escape.

It was not intended that Democracy should consist in a name merely. It was planned to produce results necessary to the well-being of man. It had four principal objects in view: The elevation of the lowly; the extension of the area of freedom; the defence of the Union; and the advancement of the glory of the country.

The Constitution declares that "no title of nobility shall be granted by the United States." This was necessary to maintain the nation's declaration of human equality. It places capital and labor upon a perfect level as to the honors of office and the consideration of Government. In the eye of our organic law, the child of toil, in coarse garments, dripping with the sweat of the brow, holds equal rank with him who clothes himself in purple and fine linen, and fares sumptuously every day. Our Brodericks are as noble as the Slidells. As long as Democracy had the fullness of life and beauty, its banner bore aloft this benevolent idea, and under them its proudest victories were achieved. Neither convention nor meeting could assemble without an outpouring of affection for, and expressions of determination to stand by, the interests of "the toiling millions." The alien and sedition laws were condemned as odious, and repealed, because they violated a right of the masses, that of free speech, and invested the officer with a sanctity incompatible with the American notion that the lowest citizen and the highest were entitled to equal immunities and protection. The Bank of the United States was destroyed, not so much upon the ground of its unconstitutionality, as that of its danger to the laboring classes. President Jackson's main argument was addressed to industry, and his triumph was achieved through the agency of that interest to which he thus appealed. His Democracy did not lead him to believe that the rich should be made richer, and the poor poorer; but rather that the weak should not be placed at the mercy of the strong, or labor be made a prey to capital. The conclusion was both sensible and humane. A large majority of every people fail to reach a condition of wealth, and as "power is always stealing from the many to the few," it is "the many," and not "the few," whose welfare ought to be especially guarded. Where now is the Democracy, my humble friend, that takes its stand by your side in your exhaustion, or your unjust deprivations, and calls upon you to be of good cheer, that you shall be invigorated and recompensed? Ah! where is it? Point me to it, if possible. Where is it found, in organization or association? It was, but is not. The assumption of the tyrant, that "capital should own labor;" that poor white men are servile, and ought to be bound in fetters; that they and their wives and children should be held as the negro is held, to be sold and debased and polluted and scourged, has so infused itself into the modern Democracy as to metamorphose all its aims, and make it the instrument of despotism. It is now effectually managed by the owner of the black man, so as to enable him to possess himself unrighteously of our inheritances, the free Territories of the country, and to force us, through spoliation, into the same beastly condition as his slaves.

It is within the recollection of most, if not all of us, that the Democracy was loud in its demands for extensions of the "area of freedom," that its blessings might be the more widely enjoyed. We then understood the policy to be for the benefit of the foreigner and our own surplus population. Now, we know the effort is continually being made, by all means, lawful and unlawful, to acquire territory for the growth of slavery alone. The most talented and influential Democratic leaders are engaged, directly or indirectly, in this work, without a murmur from any one bearing their party name. Worse than this, if possible, the more powerful wing of the Democracy insist that under the Constitution of our Government, brought forth in a hatred of oppression and a love of liberty, slavery cannot be excluded from any soil we may own or may hereafter acquire; and the other wing, in substance, reply: "We 'don't exactly know how this may be; we await 'the settlement of the question by a court 'having a common feeling and common interest with you; and if you gain a decision, we 'promise that it shall be enforced promptly 'and faithfully." President Jackson, as a coordinate branch of the Government, applied the Constitution as he understood it, and he was an accredited Democrat in his day; Judge Douglas, a Senator of the United States, would interpret the Constitution as others understand it, without weighing their passions and prejudices. Jackson and Douglas! Hyperion and Satyr! Democracy, from the beginning of the Government down to the years 1847–'48, admitted and exercised the right to exclude slavery from the Territories. Now, Democracy denies that same right most emphatically, or at least doubts it. How very imperfectly our fathers must have understood their own workmanship. They framed the fundamental law, yet had but a slight conception of its meaning. It was reserved to their puny offspring to tell us what they intended. Let us rest assured of this, and trust to history to prove its truth, that, whilst the ancient Democracy survived, the Constitution was so read as to favor freedom and free men; but, that by the modern Democracy, born of the brain of John C. Calhoun, it is, and will continue to be, so distorted as to encourage the spread of slavery.

The Union, always esteemed by every Democratic patriot as the bulwark of our liberties, is now threatened with immediate destruction by those who claim to be the elect custodians of Democratic principles. With an insulting arrogance, they lay claim to unlimited rule, without regard to the wishes of the majority or the guaranties of law, upon the ignoble pretext that it is indispensable to the cause of human bondage. In this way, we are to be brought to submit to the usurpation of a minority, in order that those who would lay unholy hands upon the altar may be bribed to keep the peace. If the people of the United States shall elect a President not approved by the South, or a portion of the South, we are informed that he shall never be inaugurated, and that the Confederacy will be at an end. These Democrats do not conceal their protocols; they placard their concerted treason, and would affright us by their very recklessness. Do they know us? Are we indeed so craven as to pale and tremble before such Heaven-defying outrage? How courses Northern blood, from Northern hearts, through Northern veins, at such a vaunt? If we deserve to live, we will dare to die in such a conflict as they would force upon us. Upon what field, in the battle for the right, did Northern courage ever fail? Not on sterile plains, or by the margin of stagnant streams, but in the pure bracing air, live the real armies of the nation, and "woe, woe to the riders that trample them down."

Our Northern people will neither avoid nor violate any obligation resting upon them. They have ever treated their Southern brethren, not only with justice, but with extreme magnanimity, and they will continue to do so voluntarily. But let aggressors beware the day when force or violence shall be resorted to, to drive the North into concessions. When that crisis shall come upon them, they will meet it as they ought to meet it, and the now-perplexing questions of slavery extension and slavery domination on this continent will be settled forever.

Perhaps the most deplorable effect of the change of principle and policy, of which I speak, is upon the character of the country. Both history and tradition sufficiently indicate the intention of the former Democracy to gain for our Government the good opinion of the world. This they hoped to do by making it strong and equitable. Its security was not to rest upon alliances, nor, indeed, upon its arms, so much as upon its strict conformity to the most rigid rules of right. It was planned for a model, and the earlier Administrations never lost sight of this fact, and they regulated their action accordingly. It had its origin in, and was long conducted on, the broadest philanthropy. It was designed to attract both the attention and the affections of mankind. The general condition of our race everywhere was one of abject subjection; the laudable purpose was, to elevate that condition. Liberty had no local habitation; her temple was to be firmly erected here. In other countries, authority was centred upon what was presumptuously called a God-selected one, or few; here it was to be extended to the God-equalized many, or all. In short, our nation was to be "an asylum for the oppressed." What would the recent Democracy make it? It has no longer anything to say of "equal and exact justice," and is entirely careless of the moral sentiment of a widely-extended Christianity. It has no desire to merit encomiums from the wise and good. It has no heart to feel, and consequently would not make sacrifices for, the general welfare. To it, liberty and slavery are but names, not existences; and integrity and injury, and virtue and vice, insensible expressions. With it, brotherhood consists in elevated condition, not in the attributes of mankind; and law is not to strengthen the weak to resist, but the strong to invade. Unchecked, it would carry us back to the barbarism of the dark ages. Alas, who should care to bear the title of Democrat, at such a cost to him as a citizen of Republican America!

> "O judgment, thou art fled to brutish beasts,
> And men have lost their reason."

The conclusion I would draw from what I have said, is, that Democracy, in the days of its glory, was the nurse of liberty and the guardian of freemen, but that it has sunk down to be but the tool of a tyrant and a parent of slaves.

Fellow citizens, let me make an appeal, not so much *to* you, as *for* our common country. There can be no nationality without law; and ours rests upon the double basis of Constitution and statute. The structure cannot be preserved by undermining its foundations. As our security is by virtue of government, and our government by virtue of law, we can only prosper as long as we maintain the supremacy of law. To lay ruthless hands upon it would be not only to destroy our own peace, but to make ourselves "a by-word and a reproach." Our honor demands our fidelity; if once parted with, it may not be easily regained,

> "For Fame's a Carthage not so soon rebuilt."

Many wait but for an excuse to blot out our most sacred charter; let them not have it in any examples of ours. Let us do our whole duty, and, whilst doing it, publish our warnings, to those who are not so exact. Let us, mildly and kindly, remind them of the bearing of a Democratic chief towards a disloyal State, and, adopting the language of his resolve, "The Federal Union—it must be preserved," stand in defence of law—the law of the Constitution, and the law of God.

There is an immortality of infamy, as well as an immortality of glory; and it has happened that whilst the wicked were reaping the one, children have been ready to inherit the other. The same night that Herostratus fired the temple of Artemis at Ephesus, Alexander the Great was born in Pella. So, at the moment when profane men shall kindle flames in the citadel of liberty, consigning themselves to everlasting disgrace, heroes, the second Washingtons, will arise to receive universal homage.

Have no fears for the future, but be prepared for it. There are clouds in the South, but if they hold the lightning, it will be discharged there, not here. The virtue, intelligence, and valor, which gave us a nation, will preserve it to a distant and grateful posterity.

REPUBLICAN PLATFORM,

Adopted by the Chicago Convention, May 17, 1860.

Resolved, That we, the delegated representatives of the Republican Electors of the United States, in Convention assembled, in discharge of the duty we owe to our constituents and our country, unite in the following declarations:

First. That the history of the nation during the last four years has fully established the propriety and necessity of the organization and perpetuation of the Republican party, and that the causes which called it into existence are permanent in their nature, and now, more than ever before, demand its peaceful and constitutional triumph.

Second. That the maintenance of the principles promulgated in the Declaration of Independence, and embodied in the Federal Constitution, "that all men are created equal; that they are endowed by their Creator with certain unalienable rights; that among these are life, liberty, and the pursuit of happiness; that to secure these rights, Governments are instituted among men, deriving their just powers from the consent of the governed," is essential to the preservation of our republican institutions; and that the Federal Constitution, the rights of the States, and the Union of the States, must and shall be preserved.

Third. That to the Union of the States this nation owes its unprecedented increase in population; its surprising development of material resources; its rapid augmentation of wealth; its happiness at home and its honor abroad; and we hold in abhorrence all schemes for disunion, come from whatever source they may; and we congratulate the country that no Republican member of Congress has uttered or countenanced the threats of disunion, so often made by Democratic members without rebuke and with applause from their political associates; and we denounce those threats of disunion, in case of a popular overthrow of their ascendency, as denying the vital principles of a free Government, and as an avowal of contemplated reason, which it is the imperative duty of an indignant people sternly to rebuke and forever silence.

Fourth. That the maintenance inviolate of the rights of the States, and especially the right of each State to order and control its own domestic institutions, according to its own judgment exclusively, is essential to that balance of power on which the perfection and endurance of our political fabric depends; and we denounce the lawless invasion by armed force of the soil of any State or Territory, no matter under what pretext, as among the gravest of crimes.

Fifth. That the present Democratic Administration has far exceeded our worst apprehensions in its measureless subserviency to the exactions of a sectional interest, as especially evidenced in its desperate exertions to force the infamous Lecompton Constitution upon the protesting people of Kansas—in construing the personal relation between master and servant to involve an unqualified property in persons—in its attempted enforcement everywhere, on land and sea, through the intervention of Congress and of the Federal courts, of the extreme pretensions of a purely local interest, and in its general and unvarying abuse of the power intrusted to it by a confiding people.

Sixth. That the people justly view with alarm the reckless extravagance which pervades every department of the Federal Government; that a return to rigid economy and accountability is indispensable to arrest the systematic plunder of the public Treasury by favored partisans; while the recent startling developments of frauds and corruptions at the Federal metropolis show that an entire change of Administration is imperatively demanded.

Seventh. That the new dogma that the Constitution of its own force carries slavery into any or all of the Territories of the United States, is a dangerous political heresy, at variance with the explicit provisions of that instrument itself, with cotemporaneous exposition, and with legislative and judicial precedent; is revolutionary in its tendency, and subversive of the peace and harmony of the country.

Eighth. That the normal condition of all the territory of the United States is that of Freedom; that as our republican fathers, when they had abolished slavery in all our national territory, ordained that "no person should be deprived of life, liberty, or property, without due process of law," it becomes our duty, by legislation, whenever such legislation is necessary, to maintain this provision of the Constitution against all attempts to violate it; and we deny the authority of Congress, of a Territorial Legislature, or of any individuals, to give legal existence to slavery in any Territory of the United States.

Ninth. That we brand the recent reopening of the African slave trade, under the cover of our national flag, aided by perversions of judicial power, as a crime against humanity, and a burning shame to our country and age; and we call upon Congress to take prompt and efficient measures for the total and final suppression of that execrable traffic.

Tenth. That in the recent vetoes by their Federal Governors of the acts of the Legislatures of Kansas and Nebraska, prohibiting slavery in those Territories, we find a practical illustration of the boasted Democratic principle of non-intervention and popular sovereignty embodied in the Kansas-Nebraska bill, and a demonstration of the deception and fraud involved therein.

Eleventh. That Kansas should of right be immediately admitted as a State under the Constitution recently formed and adopted by her people, and accepted by the House of Representatives.

Twelfth. That while providing revenue for the support of the General Government by duties upon imports, sound policy requires such an adjustment of these imposts as to encourage the development of the industrial interest of the whole country; and we commend that policy of national exchanges which secures to the working men liberal wages, to agriculture remunerating prices, to mechanics and manufacturers an adequate reward for their skill, labor, and enterprise, and to the nation commercial prosperity and independence.

Thirteenth. That we protest against any sale or alienation to others of the public lands held by actual settlers, and against any view of the free homestead policy which regards the settlers as paupers or supplicants for public bounty; and we demand the passage by Congress of the complete and satisfactory homestead measure which has already passed the House.

Fourteenth. That the Republican party is opposed to any change in our naturalization laws, or any State legislation by which the rights of citizenship hitherto accorded to immigrants from foreign lands shall be abridged or impaired; and in favor of giving a full and efficient protection to the rights of all classes of citizens, whether native or naturalized, both at home and abroad.

Fifteenth. That appropriations by Congress for river and harbor improvements of a national character, required for the accommodation and security of an existing commerce, are authorized by the Constitution and justified by an obligation of the Government to protect the lives and property of its citizens.

Sixteenth. That a railroad to the Pacific Ocean is imperatively demanded by the interests of the whole country; that the Federal Government ought to render immediate and efficient aid in its construction; and that, as preliminary thereto, a daily overland mail should be promptly established.

Seventeenth. Finally, having thus set forth our distinctive principles and views, we invite the co-operation of all citizens, however differing on other questions, who substantially agree with us, in their affirmance and support.

The Republican Executive Congressional Committee are prepared to furnish the following Speeches and Documents:

Eight Pages, 50 cents per hundred.

The State of the Country—W. H. Seward.
"Irrepressible Conflict"—W. H. Seward.
Free Homes for Free Men—G. A. Grow.
Shall the Territories be Africanized—James Harlan.
Who have Violated Compromises—John Hickman.
Invasion of Harper's Ferry—B. F. Wade.
The Speakership—G. W. Scranton and J. H. Campbell.
Colonization and Commerce—F. P. Blair.
General Politics—Orris S. Ferry.
The Demands of the South—The Republican Party Vindicated—Abraham Lincoln.
The Homestead Bill—Its Friends and its Foes—W. Windom.
The Barbarism of Slavery—Owen Lovejoy.
The New Dogma of the South—"Slavery a Blessing"—H. L. Dawes.
The Position of Parties—R. H. Duell.
The Homestead Bill—M. S. Wilkinson.
Polygamy in Utah—D. W. Gooch.
Douglas and Popular Sovereignty—Carl Schurz.
Lands for the Landless—A Tract.
The Poor Whites of the South—The Injury done them by Slavery—A Tract.
A Protective Tariff Necessary—Rights of Labor—James H. Campbell.
The Fanaticism of the Democratic Party—Owen Lovejoy.
Mission of Republicans—Sectionalism of Modern Democracy—Robert McKnight.
Southern Sectionalism—John Hickman.
Freedom vs. Slavery—John Hutchins.
Republican Land Policy—Homes for the Million—Stephen C. Foster.
Tariff—Justin S. Morrill.
Legislative Protection to the Industry of the People—Alexander H. Rice.
Modern Democracy—Henry Waldron.
The Territorial Slave Policy; The Republican Party; What the North has to do with Slavery—Thomas D. Eliot.
The Supreme Court of the United States—Roscoe Conkling.
Designs of the Republican Party—Christopher Robinson.
Address—Montgomery Blair.
The Necessity of Protecting American Labor—J. P. Verree.
The Republican Party and its Principles—James T. Hale.
Revenue and Expenditures—John Sherman.
The Claims of Agriculture—John Carey.
Negro Equality—The Right of One Man to Hold Property in Another—The Democratic Party a Disunion Party—The Success of the Republican Party the only Salvation for the Country—Benjamin Stanton.
Mutual Interest of the Farmer and Manufacturer—Carey A. Trimble.
The Tariff—Its Constitutionality, Necessity, and Advantages—John T. Nixon.
Position of Parties and Abuses of Power—Reuben E. Fenton.
Bill and Report Repealing the Territorial Laws of New Mexico—John A. Bingham.
Democracy *alias* Slavery—James B. McKean.
Abraham Lincoln, His Personal History and Public Record—E. B. Washburne.
The President's Message—The Sectional Party—John A. Bingham.
The Republican Party a Necessity—Charles F. Adams.
The Filibustering Policy of the Sham Democracy—J. J. Perry.
Modern Democracy—Justin S. Morrill.
Equality of Rights in the Territories—Harrison G. Blake.
Resigning His Position as Chairman of the Committee on Commerce and reasons for leaving the Democratic Party—Hannibal Hamlin.
Public Expenditures—R. H. Duell.
The Republican Party and the Republican Candidate for the Presidency—W. McKee Dunn.
The Republican Platform—E. G. Spaulding.
Frauds in Naval Contracts—John Sherman.
The Rights of Labor—J. K. Moorhead.
The Tariff—Seward and Cameron.
Political Issues and Presidential Candidates—John Hickman. Delivered in Philadelphia.
Principles and Purposes of the Republican Party—J. B. Alley.
Slavery: What it was, what it has done, what it intends to do—C. B. Tompkins.
Disorganization and Disunion—E. McPherson.

Sixteen Pages, $1 per hundred.

Seizure of Arsenals at Harper's Ferry, Va., and Liberty, Mo.—Lyman Trumbull.
Property in the Territories—B. F. Wade.
True Democracy—History Vindicated—C. H. Van Wyck.
Territorial Slave Code—H. Wilson.
Slavery in the Territories—John P. Hale.
"Posting the Books between the North and the South"—J. J. Perry.
The Calhoun Revolution—Its Basis and its Progress—J. R. Doolittle.
The Republican Party the Result of Southern Aggression—C. B. Sedgwick.
Admission of Kansas—M. J. Parrott.
Federalism Unmasked—Daniel R. Goodloe.
The Slavery Question—C. C. Washburn.
Thomas Corwin's Great Speech, Abridged.
The Issues—The Dred Scott Decision—The Parties—Israel Washburn, Jun.
Tariff—Samuel S. Blair.
The Rise and Fall of the Democratic Party—K. S. Bingham.
In Defence of the North and Northern Laborers—H. Hamlin.
Homesteads: The Republicans and Settlers against Democracy and Monopoly—A Tract.

Twenty-four Pages, $1.50 per hundred.

The Ruin of the Democratic Party—the Reports of the Covode and other Committees—A Tract.
Slavery in the Territories—Jacob Collamer.

Thirty-two Pages, $2 per hundred.

Thomas Corwin's Great Speech.
Success of the Calhoun Revolution: The Constitution Changed and Slavery Nationalized by the Usurpations of the Supreme Court—James M. Ashley.
The Barbarism of Slavery—Charles Sumner.

GERMAN.

Eight Pages, 50 cents per hundred.

The Demands of the South—The Republican Party Vindicated—Abraham Lincoln.
Free Homes for Free Men—G. A. Grow.
Shall the Territories be Africanized—James Harlan.
Who have Violated Compromises—John Hickman.
The Homestead Bill—Its Friends and its Foes—W. Windom
Douglas and Popular Sovereignty—Carl Schurz.
The Homestead Bill—M. S. Wilkinson.
The Barbarism of Slavery—Owen Lovejoy.
Southern Sectionalism—John Hickman.
Equality of Rights in the Territories—Harrison G. Blake.
The Claims of Agriculture—John Carey.
The Republican Party a Necessity—Charles F. Adams.
Mutual Interest of the Farmer and Manufacturer—Carey A Trimble.
Political Issues and Presidential Candidates—John Hickman Delivered in Philadelphia.

Sixteen Pages, $1 per hundred.

Seizure of the Arsenals at Harper's Ferry, Va., and Liberty Mo., and in Vindication of the Republican Party—Lyman Trumbull.
The State of the Country—W. H. Seward.
Lands for the Landless—A Tract.
Election of Speaker—H. Winter Davis.

Forty Pages, $2.50 per hundred.

The Barbarism of Slavery—Charles Sumner.

COMMITTEE.—Preston King, N. Y., *Chairman*. J. W. Grimes, Iowa, L. F. S. Foster, Conn., *on the part of the Senate* John Covode, Penn., *Treasurer*, E. G. Spaulding, N. Y., J. B. Alley, Mass., David Kilgore, Ind., J. L. N. Stratton, N. J., *on the part of the House of Reps.*

Address the Chairman, or GEORGE HARRINGTON, *Secretary.*

WASHINGTON, D. C.

POPULAR SOVEREIGNTY—THE WILL OF THE MAJORITY AGAINST THE RULE OF A MINORITY.

SPEECH

OF

HON. J. HICKMAN, OF PENNSYLVANIA,

IN THE HOUSE OF REPRESENTATIVES, JANUARY 28, 1858.

The House being in the Committee of the Whole on the state of the Union—

Mr. HICKMAN said:

Mr. CHAIRMAN: I should not have sought the floor at this time, but for the fact that silence would leave my views liable to an unpleasant misconstruction. I was an early, earnest, and sincere advocate of Mr. Buchanan's election to the Presidency of the United States, believing that his elevation would largely promote the present peace and lasting welfare of my country. His life had been a public one, and his character was that of an educated statesman and a just man. I esteemed him as eminently worthy of the largest confidence and warmest regard of the American people, as I could not doubt his Administration would alike reflect his wisdom, experience, and nice appreciation of justice; and that under it the rights of the people, of *all* the people, would be scrupulously regarded. I did not expect infallibility in his management of public affairs, and do not now expect it; and when I shall meet with what I may regard as error, I trust to be pardoned for the frankness with which I shall always proclaim my opinions.

Until I heard the annual message read, I had expected to be able to yield to its doctrines an honest and decided support; but from its Kansas policy I must strongly dissent. I am unable to give it my support. I regret exceedingly the tendency of the Executive recommendation, which, to my mind, is to place the President in a position of antagonism to the majority in Kansas. It leads to an issue between power on the one hand, and the people on the other. In such a case, I never can hesitate in determining whose cause I shall espouse, or what verdict I ought to render. I am not unmindful of the fact that the former is quite as likely to triumph with the wrong as the latter with the right; and that the ambitious may well hesitate when resolves on success are to decide for whom to do battle. The great influence of executive patronage; the full extent of executive power in this country is but feebly comprehended. We are apt to underrate it vastly. If unscrupulously exercised, it becomes a crushing despotism, as indefensible as that controlled by the greatest of tyrants—combinations can seldom resist it, individuals never. But these considerations, clearly as they have presented themselves to my mind, can never induce me to espouse a political heresy.

But the great danger surrounding our institutions does not so much arise from a want of public virtue as general intelligence. Few outside of public life watch narrowly the conduct of their public servants, and fewer still are sufficiently conversant with the machinery of Government clearly to comprehend the bearing of particular acts. If it were otherwise, high officers of Government would be less powerful for evil, and public rights more practically defensible. If, therefore, at any time, resistance to a gross and unpardonable outrage upon an admitted principle, shall prove unavailing, let not the offense, on that account, be baptized and sanctified; let it rather be an evidence of the truth of my declaration, and a warning to those who are unwilling to part with the sovereignty of the citizen.

My opposition to the President's treatment of Kansas affairs does not arise from hostility to slavery; it stands upon a foundation, the strength of which will be more generally admitted. I rest my resistance upon the violations of declared principles, of solemn pledges, and the guarantees to the nation. To ask me to sanction them, with my views, is to insult me by suspicions of my integrity. Others may act differently, it is not my province to judge them.

"I may stand alone,
But would not change my free thoughts for a throne."

I am not blind to the fact that a very different motive will be assigned for my action. I have too often seen it attributed to others, not to anticipate it in my own case. But it has become a stale cry, and, I think, must soon prove a barren one. If differing from my southern friends on any point which immediately or remotely affects the interests of slavery must subject me to anathema, so be it; I must bear up under it; I cannot deny my convictions that I may receive a charitable judgment.

I do not oppose slavery where it legally exists. It is there a matter between the master and the slave; it concerns them alone; and I will not interfere with it or them. I yield a ready allegiance to our common Constitution, and will support all the laws made under it as long as they remain in force, to whatever subject they may relate, or whatever burdens they may impose upon me. But when any man, or body of men, seek to plant that institution or any other on my soil, or where I have the legal right to speak, I will then exercise the prerogative of a freeman. And when this is attempted by force or by fraud, when it is manifested in an utter disregard and profound contempt for the popular will, that, of itself, will induce me to resist it to the last.

This is a law to me—and there is no other sound law of liberty—to exercise all my rights in their fullness, and to grant the same measure of power to my neighbor. The application of this rule of action is not only good for individuals, but equally so for communities and States. It is a golden rule; it is a pure constitutional rule. The North must regard all the rights of the South, and the South must regard all the rights of the North—in the States and in the Territories—throughout the broad land—for neither wears a panoply against the assaults of the other. There are two classes of persons, however, who, in a marked manner, interfere with this course of conduct. They are those who *deny* and those who *grant* all demands made, whether just or unjust. Extremists in the South, judging all northern men to be of the former class, designate them as enemies and Abolitionists; and certain northern politicians looking upon a few northern Democrats as a type of the whole, have declared Democracy to be the ally of slavery. Both cannot be right, and believe that they are equally wrong. Denying, as I do, the charge that Democracy has entered into a league with slavery, I am yet willing to admit, as I have said, the existence of a few northern confederates with it. I do not believe them able to exercise much power, whatever their disposition. If it shall prove otherwise in their action upon the present question, I must leave to them the responsibilities of a course destructive of the effective force of our party organization.

I think I may, with great truth, say that the enactment of the law organizing the Territories of Kansas and Nebraska, including the repeal of the Missouri compromise, was not, originally, a popular movement at the North. It was regarded with suspicion, and believed to be impolitic if not unjust. Mr. Buchanan himself, by expressing the wish, in his Reading letter, that that line should be extended to the Pacific ocean, gave to the compromise a sanctity or popularity additional to that derived from thirty-four years' acquiescence; and when its contemplated destruction was announced, it was received with great astonishment and deep regret. It was honestly believed, by very many, to be a movement to advance the peculiar interests of the South at the expense of those for whose benefit the territory north of the line had been dedicated to freedom. The doctrine of popular sovereignty by which it was accompanied, made it at first but tolerable, though, eventually, palatable. Could the future history of Kansas have then been read, as it has since transpired to this moment; the repeated frauds and usurpations practiced and imposed upon her people; her agonizing and fruitless cries for justice; the cruel and crushing sympathy of high Federal officers with her oppressors; her appeal for free institutions derided by ruffians, and slavery fastened upon her in bold defiance of her rights; could all this have been foreseen, the northern advocate of that legislation could not have breasted for a single moment the withering tornado such wrongs would have raised against him. These unjust consequences, not naturally flowing from the legislation spoken of, have now resulted; and if they would not have been tolerated then, why should they be now? Have we an overplus of political power which should induce us to carry so exhausting a burden with patience? Once taken up by the party they would cling to it like the Man of the Mountain to the back of the sailor, choking it and sinking it to the earth. It is too soon for us to forget what overpowering strength we brought to the polls in 1852, and the means—yes, sir, the means—by which it was recklessly frittered away before 1856.

Mr. Chairman, I am upon a point I feel deeply, and if I shall express myself with warmth and decision I must be pardoned. As long as I am capable of appreciating truth, I can never lend myself to the attempt now being made, with high sanctions, to undermine the foundation upon which the modern territorial legislation rests, and to falsify pledges upon the faith of which the last presidential election was accomplished. The vital principle, the soul of the Nebraska-Kansas bill, is to be blasted. The majority are not necessarily to rule. If I can read recent events at all, I learn so much from them. Let the people understand this; teach them the whole truth, and then hear their response. Think you the mighty millions of the North, the East, and the West will be quieted as children by baubles? Will they allow legislation to be construed one way to-day, and enforced a different way to-morrow? In short, will they submit always to stake upon a game where they never can win? If they are so miserably made up, so destitute of real manhood, they are truly only fit to be the "white slaves" of whom we have occasionally heard, and from my soul I pity them. The name of freeman fits them not, but hangs upon them,

> ——— "like a giant's robe
> Upon a dwarfish thief."

My course is my own; others are not answerable for it; and I would not implicate them in my action if I could. But I will resist every attempt, no matter from what quarter it may come, to inflict a despotism upon the people of Kansas, when the law guaranties them liberty, or to impinge upon the promises the Democracy took upon themselves to make in the last presidential campaign.

The recommendation in the message goes out as "a forlorn hope" against what has heretofore been supposed to be the strongly intrenched doctrine of popular sovereignty. What will the country do, is the question. Will it defend this great principle in the hour of its severe trial? Or will it allow the right of self-government to be successfully assaulted? Has it already become an obsolete, a worn-out thing? But two years ago I expressed the opinion that those most prominently instrumental in causing the Democratic party to be pledged to maintain the doctrine of popular sovereignty, in the organization of our Territories, would deeply regret it. I never doubted that it would operate against the growth of the South. On the 19th of March, 1856, when insisting upon an investigation into alleged election frauds in Kansas, I had occasion to use these words:

"Sir, the supporters of that bill [the Nebraska-Kansas bill] have proclaimed to the nation that the Territories of the United States are to constitute 'a fair field,' and that there is to be 'a free fight' there, between the North and the South, to decide whether slavery or freedom shall rule them. If the energy, the enterprise, the active modes of life, the available capital, and the numbers of the North, shall not be able to compete successfully with their opposites in the South, and secure freedom to the Territories, then I will admit that there is a vitality and a power in slavery which we of the North have never dreamed of. In my opinion, the Representatives of the South in the Thirty-Third Congress 'have sown the fire, and they will gather fire into their own garners.'"

The prediction is fulfilled; for now, like Pyrene, the Iberian princess, they fly in fear from their own child; it is a serpent, and pursues them. The day of repentance has come upon them much sooner than I anticipated. Instead of decades, it has required but brief months to inculcate the lesson which should never be forgotten, that weakness cannot long triumph over strength, nor minorities, in this free land, trample down majorities. If what we have esteemed the great truths of republican government are not a sheer lie, then squatter sovereignty, adequately protected, will give the virgin lands of our Confederacy to the free white man, and not the negro slave. This is now seen, and sovereignty is *not* to be protected; it is to be crushed out; by unwarrantable, illegal interference it is to be crushed out; and the hitherto pliant North is expected to acquiesce. If it submits, be it so. I will, never! no, never!

A southern writer in De Bow's Weekly Press exhibits in a striking light the imperative necessity resting upon the South to make Kansas a slave State. It is declared to be the necessity arising from self-preservation, and such as originates the highest law. I read an extract from the article referred to, of the date of January 16, 1858:

"The surrender of Kansas to the operation of the majority rule, under the cry of popular sovereignty in the Territories, without constitutional warrant, and her absorption by the non-slaveholding power of the country, would make the evil of the times no longer prospective, but instant and imminent. By the fact of this surrender, the South would become subordinant, and the North predominant, in the Union. Never again, in the Union, could the equilibrium of State sovereign representation between the South and the North be either maintained in or restored to the Senate. Never again, in the Union, could the equality of the South with the North be either maintained in or restored to the House of Representatives. No further barrier could be constructed between either the aggressive territorial or political rapacity of the North, and the weakened and diminished South. No other bulwark could be raised to guard either the moral or social integrity of the South against the disrupting and destructive legal and social systems of the North. The South, like Hector bound to the car of Achilles, would soon be dragged by the triumphant North around a ruined possession, quickly to be followed by the erasive plowshare of the invading conqueror.

"The loss of Kansas to the South would involve the loss of Missouri; and the loss of Missouri would destroy the moral as well as political prestige of the South, and invade the integrity of their institutions. The moral prestige of States, like that of individuals, once destroyed, no earthly power can restore; and the integrity of State establishments, like the chastity of woman, once subjected to invasion, continues at the will of the despoiler. With abolitionized Iowa stretching along the northern boundary of Missouri, and abolitionized Kansas covering her western boundary, whilst there poured into her bosom, through Iowa and Kansas, from the more inhospitable lake and northern Atlantic regions, a continuous stream of agrarian radicals of any and all parties in those regions, alike determined to obtain control of her government, and to assert the rule of the majority in the line of emancipation, slave property in Missouri would become too precarious in its tenure to be holden, and the necessity for its sale or removal would at once arise. It may be confidently asserted that, under these circumstances, in five years Missouri would cease to be a slaveholding State. Already, in view of the anticipated result, Abolition journals have been started in Missouri, and candidates for Congress have unfurled the banner of emancipation."

But, Mr. Chairman, I wish to be more particular and precise in my objections to that part of the President's message to which I have made reference, and to the admission of Kansas into the Union on the Lecompton constitution. They arise—

First. From the antagonism of that policy and measure to what has been called the great republican principle of the Nebraska-Kansas bill; and

Second. From the attempts making to violate the plighted faith of the Democratic party.

"The true intent and meaning" of the act organizing the Territory of Kansas, is declared to be "to leave the people thereof perfectly free to form and regulate their domestic institutions in their own way." This language would seem too unequivocal to be overcome by the most abstruse diplomatist, or the most adroit hair-splitting politician. No doubt, I suggest, is allowed to remain as to "the true intent and meaning" of the enactment. It was to give full, perfect, unrestricted sovereignty to the people of Kansas. It is this right, thus clearly given to them, the inhabitants of the Territory now claim; nothing more, nothing less.

But I understand the President to say that they are careless about all questions to be settled by their fundamental law, except the single one of negro slavery. Who conferred upon this officer the authority to speak so confidently for the people of Kansas? Surely Congress never did; for they have, by an unrepealed law, vested all power in the people alone; and if the people have intrusted him with an agency, it is proper he should show his warrant. This, most unfortunately, and of course most unintentionally, tends to indorse and sustain that organized, systematic attempt, long insisted upon and persevered in, to stifle the popular voice in the Territory, and to cast its government into the hands of those having no shadow of right to exercise it. Free government is not to be allowed, because the people will not consult the wishes of the Platte district, nor accept institutions attempted to be forced on them from abroad. The language of the President is somewhat peculiar, and, to my mind, singularly unsound. He says:

"The convention were not bound by its terms [the terms of the Nebraska-Kansas bill] to submit any other portion of the instrument [the constitution] to an election, except that which relates to the 'domestic institution' of slavery. This will be rendered clear by a simple reference to its language. It was 'not to legislate slavery into any Territory or State, nor to exclude it therefrom, but to leave the people thereof perfectly free to form and regulate their domestic institutions in their own way.' According to the plain construction of the sentence, the words 'domestic institutions' have a direct, as they have an appropriate reference to slavery. 'Domestic institutions' are limited to the family. The relation between master and slave, and a few others, are 'domestic institutions,' and are entirely distinct from institutions of a political character. Besides, there was no question then before Congress, nor indeed has there since been any serious question before the people of Kansas or the country, except that which relates to the 'domestic institution' of slavery."

All the obligations which "rested on the Lecompton convention to submit their constitution to an election" he assumes to be derived from the act of Congress. He contends that "domestic institutions," being synonymous with slavery, it is therefore not required to submit any other matter to the popular decision. Let us test this remarkable view by carrying it to its consequences. If "domestic institutions" mean merely slavery, then it is clear that the power given to the people "to form and regulate their domestic institutions in their own way," confers only the power "to form and regulate" slavery "in their own way." But this conclusion would prove too great an absurdity for its advocates to profit by. The policy of the Government with reference to slavery in the Territories, was intended to be permanently settled by the Nebraska-Kansas bill, giving to the people thereof complete sovereignty over all their institutions. All power to legislate on the subject of slavery was denied to Congress and given to the people of the Territory. Congress declared it was—

"The true intent and meaning of that act not to legislate slavery into any Territory or State, nor to exclude it therefrom, but to leave the people thereof perfectly free to form and regulate their domestic institutions in their own way."

As I read it, and as the country has thus far interpreted it, slavery was to be left to the determination of the people of the Territory just *as all the rest of their domestic institutions.* Indeed the whole argument for the legislation referred to, proceeded upon that ground. They, the people, were to have their institutions in their own way —*all* their institutions. Their power was not large or unlimited with regard to one, and small or limited with regard to another; it was equal with respect to all. I need scarcely contend that if their will is to govern, it becomes necessary to ascertain what it is. As I look upon it, therefore, the admission that the question of slavery should be submitted to a vote of the people for the purpose of ascertaining their wishes touching that institution, carries with it the further admission that all their other institutions should be subjected to the same test. The error arises from shutting out of view the fact that the territorial legislation of 1854 intended to establish a governmental policy with respect to slavery; that it was designed to leave that "*domestic institution*" just where all other "domestic institutions" were left —within the popular control. That by using the words "slavery" and "domestic institutions" in the same sentence, Congress did not intend they should be regarded as synonymous, but as a member and a family. Slavery is a domestic institution, not domestic institutions; it is singular, not plural; it is one, not many. To adopt this fault of interpretation, would be to do not only great, and perhaps irretrievable injury to the people of Kansas, but to those of every Territory hereafter to be organized.

Is it not too plain that popular sovereignty, so much extolled in the Thirty-Third Congress, and so highly recommended in the last presidential contest, as the sound principle upon which our Territories were thenceforth to be organized and governed—which was declared as giving all power into the hands of the people—is to be sweated down to the very moderate dimensions of a privilege to say whether they will hold a negro in bonds or not? No opinion can be expressed as to the organization of the legislative, executive, or judicial branches of the government; none of the constitutional safeguards afforded to life and liberty are of any importance to the citizen. He may not speak as to them; his whole voice is to be kept for his yea or nay on negro slavery. This is Tom Thumb sovereignty, or sovereignty in a nut-shell.

The case is even worse than I have exhibited it. Nothing has been submitted for popular determination. Slavery could not be voted down by voting the "constitution with no slavery," when the instrument expressly declares that, under such vote, "the right of property in slaves now in the Territory shall in no manner be interfered with." That right of property carries with it the increase of those slaves as completely as if born in South Carolina; and if that right "*shall not be interfered with,*" slavery must continue. I have never before been taught that that is a free State in which the negro and his issue are to be holden as slaves, and where the property in slaves "shall not be interfered with." The right of the people "to form and regulate their domestic institutions in their own way," now means simply "to form and regulate" slavery, provided they "form" it in a State, and do not "regulate" it out. This I would designate as sovereignty invisible.

This solemn mockery of a guarantied right is to be tolerated; not only tolerated, but encouraged and confirmed by the action of the present Congress, because the convention which perpetrated the enormity, represented, as I am told, the sovereignty of the people. No such reason exists. I would as soon recognize a bastard as a lawful heir, as the Lecompton convention to be the offspring of the people of Kansas. The fact that others may have recognized it as a legal body, imposes no obligation upon me to force myself to the same unwise conclusion. It is one of the fruits of a well-digested fraud concocted in the fall of 1854, and persevered in until the present moment; a fraud by which slavery was to be forced into the State when formed, without respect to the sentiment of the people. The very purpose of the fraud was to override the will of the people; to substitute the action of a minority for the rule of the majority. In organizing the Territory under the Nebraska-Kansas act, the first thing manifested was an anti-republican movement, subversive of the principles of the act, and those concerned in it took as much trouble to hide the facts as Periander did to conceal his grave, and committed as many crimes in doing so. The ballot-box gave no response to the resolves or wishes of the residents; it pointed only to treasonable acts striking at the very foundation of our institutions. Ruffianism has held uninterrupted sway there. It made legislators, who made a convention, which made a constitution. The great grandchild bears most unmistakable evidence of its parentage, and it would indeed be strange if it did not subvert the principle that the people are free "to form and regulate their domestic institutions in their own way."

"For he that once hath missed the right way,
The further he doth go the further he doth stray."

I am unwilling to marshal proofs to support the position here assumed, as the whole living history of Kansas attests its strength.

Sir, how does it happen that no man has yet been found with Democracy sound enough to bear up against the air of Kansas? Four Governors have been appointed in the space of about thirty months, from among the wisest and best of our party, and now the office is again vacant. How comes this? It finds its solution in the fact that "Democracy is morality," and unable to countenance so gross and palpable a usurpation as has always existed there. Those four high officers have all returned to us, speaking the same language, uttering the same words—that sovereignty is crushed out there. And what answer is made to this? A southern paper gives it, in declaring they are to be marked—their ears cut and tails split; they are to be read out. Take care, sir, that you do not read out the whole North. In the great political contest of 1856, how our energies were taxed to the utmost! Every vote was of importance—of vast importance—not to the North merely, but to the South—ay, to the South! How they trembled there! "Sectionalism" they thought would prevail. Looking back upon that fearful struggle, may we not well pause long enough to inquire what will probaly be the result of future battles, when soldiers are so unceremoniously shot, at a time when they can be so illy spared?

I have not forgotten the almost impenetrable gloom which overhung my own State, and consequently the whole country, during the fierce conflict to which I have alluded. It was then that the persuasive voice of one who now fills a place near the person of the President was heard in our midst, proclaiming the right of Kansas to be self-governed, and expressing his determination, as a son of the South, to carry out the will of her people. His present high position was bestowed upon him, doubtless, in consequence of the influence it was his fortune then to exercise. I fear his friends who, at that time, listened to him with so much true pleasure, were not prepared for the intelligence which just before our meeting flashed along the telegraphic wires, that the President and his Cabinet were a unit in favor of the admission of Kansas into the Union under the Lecompton constitution. But their greatest regret will, perhaps, be that they have forfeited the favorable regard of one in whose behalf they have taken so strong an interest, for the reason that they learned too well the salutary lessons he inculcated.

I cannot follow this digression further, although not unprofitable, but must resume my argument. I deny that the Lecompton convention represented the sovereignty of the people, for another reason. In the election of its members, a majority of those really entitled to vote were completely disfranchised. It was thus made to be the representative of a minority merely. In the language of Governor Walker, "it had vital, not technical, defects in the very substance of its organization under the territorial law." Out of thirty-four counties composing election districts, and in which it was requisite a census should be taken and voters registered by officers appointed by the Legislature itself, nineteen had no census taken and no representation assigned them, and fifteen had no registry of voters, and could not, therefore, vote at all. The nineteen counties were a majority of all the counties, and were unrepresented; the fifteen counties had more votes than were given to all the delegates who signed the constitution, and could not cast a single vote. How, then, can it be said that this was a convention of delegates of the people; and, as such, entitled to speak for them, act for them, and bind them? Under such circumstances, are a people left "free to form and regulate their domestic institutions in their own way?"

A further objection exists to the composition of this convention. Its members not only did not represent a majority, but those who controlled its action procured their election by a fraud. The delegates from Douglas county, including the president of the convention, suspected of a design to fasten a constitution upon the people without submitting it to them for their acceptance or rejection, issued the following card:

"*To the Democratic Voters of Douglas County:*

"It having been stated by that Abolition newspaper, the Herald of Freedom, and by some disaffected bogus Democrats, who have got up an independent ticket, for the purpose of securing the vote of the Black Republicans, that the regular nominees of the Democratic convention were opposed to submitting the constitution to the people, we, the candidates of the Democratic party, submit the following resolutions, which were adopted by the Democratic convention which placed us in nomination, and which we fully and heartily indorse, as a complete refutation of the slanders above referred to.

JOHN CALHOUN, A. W. JONES,
W. S. WELLS, H. BUTCHER,
L. S. BOLLING, JOHN M. WALLACE,
WM. T. SPICELY, L. A. PRATHER.

"LECOMPTON, KANSAS TERRITORY, *June* 13, 1857."

"*Resolved*, That we will support no man as a delegate to the constitutional convention, whose duties it will be to frame the constitution of the future State of Kansas and to mold the political institutions under which we, as a people, are to live, unless he pledges himself fully, freely, and without reservation, to use every honorable means to submit the same to every *bona fide* actual citizen of Kansas, at the proper time for the vote being taken upon the adoption by the people, in order that the said constitution may be adopted or rejected by the actual settlers in this Territory, as the majority of the voters shall decide."

These men, by this act of baseness, not only accomplished their election, but placed the convention within their own control. Am I to be taught that our institutions can only be supported by public virtue, and then asked to defend such a proceeding as I have indicated, upon the ground that it is sovereign, republican, and binding upon the citizen? This is felon sovereignty.

The injustice of the course pursued towards the people of Kansas is very distinct. They are by law empowered to form their institutions in their own way; and yet the supporters of the Lecompton convention require them to adopt particular forms to make known that will, not because the *bona fide* settlers approve of them, but because their supporters approve of them. If one tenth maintain the legislation originating the constitution, and nine tenths repudiate and condemn it, can it be said the instrument is the offspring of sovereignty? But suppose every votable inhabitant had sanctioned the call of a convention, and yet a large majority should condemn the work of such a body when finished: would not a plain, common-sense interpretation of the organic act require us to reject it? The proposition is too plain for argument. I will merely inquire what the sentiment of the people is; and when I learn that, by employing such means as are likely to reveal it, I will aid it, whether I can sanction their conclusions or not. Anything else would fall short of giving a popular government; it would be but a government of force or fraud.

I deeply regret that those who support the Lecompton constitution have not rested that support upon a principle, but upon expediency. As I read the message of the President, he sanctions it in order that the country may get rid of the excitement which has so long prevailed on the subject. What excitement, pray? That which has been caused by repeated acts of violence, smothering the popular will, and gagging the popular voice. Its language is:

"When once admitted into the Union, whether with or without slavery, the excitement beyond her own limits will speedily pass away, and she will then, for the first time, be left, as she ought to have been long since, to manage her own affairs in her own way. If her constitution on the subject of slavery, or on any other subject, be displeasing to a majority of the people, no human power can prevent them from changing it within a brief period."

In my judgment a principle should never be sacrificed to expediency. But I deny the expediency of the course recommended, and the argument to sustain it is, to my mind, unfortunate. The President says: "if her constitution on the subject of slavery, or on any other subject, be displeasing to a majority of the people, no human power can prevent them from changing it within a brief period." The organic act promises the people that they may "form and regulate their domestic institutions in their own way;" now they are told they should take a fundamental law, in the making of which they had no part, and of which they totally disapprove, because "no human power can prevent them from changing it within a brief period." Now, at the time they seek admission into the Union, oppression forces institutions upon them; but when admitted, that hand will be withdrawn and they will regain their rights. This is sovereignty with suspended animation.

In opposition to the proposed policy of forcing upon the people what they do not want, I place the Democratic doctrine of popular sovereignty, which will give to the people what they do want. The President requires us to take a new but ragged garment, and attempts to comfort us by saying it can be patched and made sound. I will never traffic in goods which are defective, and will not wear, if I know it, notwithstanding I may buy, others if I do not like them. I will never barter truths for errors, knowing that I may support the latter by sophistries. I believe, with Milton, that—

"Truth is strong! Next to the Almighty, she needs no policies, no stratagems, no licensings to make her victorious."

And I will follow her wherever she may lead. If from power, then I am against power. If from the mass, then I am against the mass. If from my friends, then I am against my friends. If into solitude and the desert, I will make her my companion forever.

The rules of the House deny me the time to pursue this branch of my argument further, however much I may desire to do so. I shall now contend that, to adopt the course recommended by the President to Congress to support the action of the Lecompton convention, would be to violate the manifold and manifest pledges of the Democratic party touching the doctrine of popular sovereignty in the Territories.

The main or principal ground taken by the Republican party has been, that the Democracy were not to be trusted on questions involving the interests of slavery, and that their management of Kansas affairs afforded the sustaining proof. It will not do for us to say that it produced no effect upon the public mind. We were constrained to admit the policy, although we denied the justice of the appeal. In Pennsylvania, within sight of Wheatland, the home of the present Chief Magistrate, an impression had been made against us. The reply was ready and potent, that Mr. Buchanan, having favored the extension of the Missouri compromise to the Pacific, had favored the exclusion of slavery from the territory north of that line, including Kansas; that he was a northern man, having, as such, sympathies with the white laborer, and likely, for that reason, to see full justice done him; that he had proved himself honest, and as the resolves of his party bound him to the doctrine of popular sovereignty, and the sentiment in Kansas was most unmistakably for a free State, there could be no doubt he would see the organic act fully and impartially carried out, and slavery repressed. Confidence was reëstablished and a Democratic victory achieved. If the recent message could have been then anticipated, I do not hesitate to express my conviction that Pennsylvania would have cast an immense majority of her votes against him. His old congressional district—a part of which I have the honor to represent—I am satisfied would have spoken in a very different voice. You know but little of the present feeling in Pennsylvania if you suppose her sons can be induced to support the views of the Executive regarding the Lecompton convention. There is an accusation of bad faith, and I confess I have felt myself unable to answer it, and consequently unwilling to attempt it.

It was not alone in Pennsylvania our party committed itself to a faithful expression of the popular wish in Kansas. North and South, throughout the States, it was pledged in the most solemn terms to the same thing. There was no conflict of political opinion in the different sections of the Union; all acknowledged the obligation of the principle of the Nebraska-Kansas bill, and all expressed their unfaltering determination to defend the sovereign will of the people, whether its expression was for freedom or slavery. That these declarations were honestly made I do not doubt; the Cincinnati platform had then but recently been constructed, and all seemed to fully understand it. The resolution, to which I more especially refer, was demanded by the South, and fully accepted by the North. This demand was occasioned, doubtless, by a fear of the former that the latter was more or less unfriendly to the new territorial legislation. The principle of this legislation was hence reasserted and embodied, and became the bond of Democratic fellowship. It is too plain for misconstruction even now:

"*Resolved*, That we recognize the right of the people of all the Territories, including Kansas and Nebraska, acting through the legally and fairly-expressed will of a majority of actual residents, and whenever the number of their inhabitants justifies it, to form a constitution, with or without domestic slavery, and be admitted into the Union upon terms of perfect equality with the other States."

It did not speak for Kansas merely but for "all the Territories." "The people of all the Territories, including Kansas and Nebraska, acting through the legally and fairly-expressed will of a majority of actual residents" are to form constitutions. And here, let me observe, that in no other way are constitutions to be formed. The resolution follows the act of Congress in indicating the mode in which constitutions are to be formed, namely, by "the people acting through the legally and fairly-expressed will of a majority of actual residents." It was thus emphatically announced that a constitution could not be given to Kansas in any but the one way. Again, I say, the party was trusted, and it triumphed.

The inaugural address of the new President evinced a clear comprehension of the grounds upon which his election had been accomplished, and a determination to observe the most perfect good faith. In speaking of the Territories its language was:

"It is the imperative and indispensable duty of the Government of the United States to secure to every resident inhabitant the free and independent expression of his opinion by his vote. This sacred right of each individual must be preserved!"

This is not a passage framed for the purpose of ambiguity; it removes all doubt, if any existed before, as to the conviction of the speaker, that "the free and independent expression of his opinion by his vote" must be secured "to every resident" of Kansas, at all times. Here was a conclusion reached; and we find the President, afterwards, consistently and persistently carrying it out. Be it remembered "the resident" of Kansas was to be secured in the "free and independent expression of his opinion by his vote." The President of the United States had so determined; and with this purpose fixed, he insisted upon the Hon. Robert J. Walker accepting from him the appointment of Governor of Kansas, to effectuate it. The reason for selecting the individual named, is to be found in the fact that there was a perfect agreement of the two as to the course to be pursued. This is most evident from the letter of Governor Walker accepting the appointment, and from the instructions issued to him. In the letter alluded to Governor Walker says:

"I understand that you and your Cabinet cordially concur in the opinion expressed by me, that the actual *bona fide* residents of the Territory of Kansas, by a fair and regular vote, unaffected by fraud or violence, must be permitted, in adopting their State constitution, to decide for themselves what shall be their social institutions. This is the great fundamental principle of the act of Congress organizing that Territory, affirmed by the Supreme Court of the United States, and is in accordance with the views uniformly expressed by me throughout my public career. I contemplate a peaceful solution of this question by an appeal to the intelligence and patriotism of the people of Kansas, who should all participate fully and freely in this decision, and by a majority of whose votes the decision must be made, as the only and constitutional mode of adjustment.

"I will go, then, and endeavor to adjust these difficulties, in the full confidence, as strongly expressed by you, that I will be sustained by all your own high authority, with the cordial coöperation of all your Cabinet."

The instructions to this officer are equally conclusive of the fact:

"The institutions of Kansas should be established by the votes of the people of Kansas, unawed and uninterrupted by force and fraud.

"When such a constitution shall be submitted to the people of the Territory, they must be protected in the exercise of their right to vote for or against the instrument, and the fair expression of the popular will must not be interrupted by fraud or violence."

But the letter and instructions, as quoted, are proof of a much more important matter than that for which I have used them, for they conclusively establish that there was then an anxious wish on the part of the President that the people of the Territory should be fully protected in the exercise of their right to vote upon their constitution. I repeat his words: "They must be protected in the exercise of *their right to vote for* or against the instrument." Not in their right to vote for or against *a part* of the instrument, but *the instrument*—the whole instrument.

The Union, the organ of the Administration, of the 7th of July last, seems fully to appreciate the ground then held by the President, and, in defending that position, gives a most satisfactory reason for assuming it. I will read an extract from that paper of the date named:

"When there is no serious dispute upon the constitution, either in the convention or among the people, the power of the delegates alone may put it in operation. But such is not the case in Kansas. The most violent struggle this country ever saw, upon the most important issue which the Constitution is to determine, has been going on there for several years, between parties so evenly balanced that both claim the majority, and so hostile to one another that numerous lives have been lost in the contest. Under these circumstances there can be no such thing as ascertaining clearly and without doubt, the will of the people in any way except by their own direct expression of it at the polls. A constitution not subjected to that test, no matter what it contains, will never be acknowledged by its opponents to be anything but a fraud." * * * * * "We do most devoutly believe that unless the constitution of Kansas be submitted to a direct vote of the people, the unhappy controversy which has heretofore raged in that Territory will be prolonged for an indefinite time to come."

It is no answer to all this to say that other States have been admitted into the Union without submitting their constitutions to a popular vote. It would not be an answer if such had been the case with each and every one of the eighteen admitted States. If there were a thousand precedent cases of States so admitted, where there was no serious dispute among the citizens as to the particular form of their institutions, they would fall short of affording an argument for the admission of one where such difficulty does exist. Kansas is a case standing by itself; it has no parallels; it is not to be illustrated by precedent. Its feature are peculiar—anomalous; and the circumstances surrounding it such as never before surrounded the inchoate State. To it popular sovereignty most specially applies. Congress, the dominant political party, the President of the United States, the Governor of the Territory, all declared the people should have just such republican institutions as they might desire. All looked to a vote of the people as the means to determine the popular will. The people now ask that such vote may indicate their wishes. All sovereignty resides in the people, and no admitted principle refuses its exercise in the mode desired. Why shall they not, then, speak at the polls?

Here I pause for a moment. In looking back from the point now reached, we see the Democratic party and the President have alike pursued a comparatively new, yet well-defined and strongly-marked policy. The Missouri compromise line, after continuing for years, is found to be too restrictive; the common territory of the nation should be open to the occupancy of our citizens in common. The Nebraska-Kansas bill is enacted, and the people of the Territories are to "*form*" as they are to "regulate" their "domestic institutions." In the North and in the South the doctrine is accepted, and eagerly they push forward their respective schemes for colonizing Kansas, for now numbers shall control the institutions there. By river and by land the emigration hastens forward, and the cabin is scarcely prepared for shelter before the struggle for power, for control, commences, and it is grasped and held by the friends of the South. It is alleged that strangers to the soil, Missouri borderers, decide the contest: the reply is, you shall not inquire as to that, or any other matter; the people rule. The hasty and surperficial observer declares the South has gained an undue advantage over the North, and a sound of exultation is heard around us and in the distance. Thus baffled in the Territories, will the North, aspiring to executive power, still adhere to that sovereignty which has failed her? She must do so, or abandon her long-cherished object. The pledge is presented to her; she accepts it boldly, and repeats to the world what the faint-hearted believe is to degrade her free-born and undaunted sons:

"We recognize the right of the people of all the Territories, including Kansas and Nebraska, acting through the legally and fairly expressed will of the majority of actual residents; and whenever the number of their inhabitants justifies it, to form a constitution, with or without domestic slavery, and be admitted into the Union upon terms of perfect equality with the other States."

There is a hand-to-hand encounter. Now, again, the cry, as one of victory, resounds throughout the land, "the will of the majority, legally and fairly expressed, shall be the law of the Territories." It is barely uttered before an attempt is made to stifle it; for in the far Northwest the South has been outcolonized, and slavery is likely to be excluded from the soil. We were not prepared for this; for if the act of a minority, or, at best, a doubtful majority, can, for the time, establish a domestic institution, an actual majority should be able to form and regulate and perpetuate other or all domestic institutions.

The Democratic party and the President were honest in their support of popular sovereignty. This was not only the case before, but after the election. On no other hypothesis can you account for their early, distinct, and repeated avowals of it. The President intended to enforce it in Kansas literally and truly. There had never been but one interpretation given to it by the party of which he was, the head, and he understood it clearly. It was, that the fundamental law, the constitution, which gave form and regulation to their institutions, all their institutions, should not be imposed upon the people until sanctioned and adopted by a vote of the majority. If such was not the case, how came it that the President did not at once repudiate the action of Governor Walker in giving assurance that the Lecompton convention must submit their constitution to a vote, or it would be rejected by Congress? How could he pass over this sentence, in the address of that officer to the people of the Territory, without notice?

"Kansas never can be brought into the Union, with or without slavery, except by a previous solemn decision, fully, freely, and fairly made by a majority of her people, in voting for or against the adoption of the State constitution."

It must be conceded that the President approved of Governor Walker's course, and that it required him to do so to make his own course consistent, and the party true to their avowals.

I here leave the discussion. I am unwilling to repeat points raised in the earlier portion of my remarks, to assist this branch of my argument, and I do not think it necessary to do so. I can only use this general expression, that, in my opinion, the course now recommended to us by the President in his message is unjust to, because inconsistent with, himself, and would, if carried out, rob the Nebraska-Kansas act of its vital principle, and stand as an accusing record against the good faith of the Democratic party, crippling it for years to come, if not destroying it for the future. In such an event, where is that strong hand which is to lay hold of the rudder and still direct the ship of State, freighted with the hopes of mankind, in her course of material greatness and increasing glory? What, in that day, will constitute the breakwater against which fanaticism shall dash in its wild fury as the hurricane may bear it from the North or the South? How will then fare the Union, with which we are everything, without which we are nothing?

Do you believe you can satisfy the country of the propriety of planting slavery on that soil, from which the Missouri compromise excluded it, upon the newest doctrine that it should be left to the laws of climate and production alone, and that neither of these will exclude it? that popular sovereignty, applied by the legislation of 1854 to the rule of the Territories of the United States, may be trampled under foot upon the pretense that forms of law have been duly observed in establishing it? that popular elections may be carried under solemn guarantees to the voter, and all pledges be broken the moment they have performed their work? that the principal may instruct the agent, and the agent, by faithfully obeying the instructions given, shall render himself obnoxious to the just indignation of his superior? that that Territory is self-governed whose highest law is made and riveted upon it by a convention in whose composition one half the Territory was unrepresented and disfranchised, which was ordained by a Legislature never acknowledged because never elected? in short, that all is well, and that principle and faith are inviolably kept in Kansas, when they know that nine tenths of her citizens, acting together, are unable to prevent the adoption of institutions which they never can acknowledge without disgrace?

Do you believe you can satisfy the country of all this? I tell you here to-day plainly that the northern Democracy never will be able to satisfy northern men of these things. Unlike the ancient knight, those who support this strange policy will be known, although they may change the color of their armor at every charge they make hereafter. The time has come at last, and not too soon, when a new requisition will be made by northern constituencies—an earnest and manly defense of northern honor and of northern rights, whilst giving the utmost demands of justice to their brethren of the South. If unpardonable to insist upon so much equality, then we have reached the end of national platforms, and the beginning of sectional Presidents—to my mind the last calamity to be survived; for then will begin those acts of aggressive interference which, leading to protracted and desolating wars, must end in establishing among children of the same blood the cruel relation of conqueror and captive.

Printed at the Congressional Globe Office.

SOUTHERN SECTIONALISM.

SPEECH

OF

HON. JOHN HICKMAN, OF PENN.

Delivered in the U. S. House of Representatives, May 1, 1860.

Mr. HICKMAN said:

Mr. CHAIRMAN: I will answer to God and my country much that has been said on the Administration side of this House. I speak of sectionalism—a subject frequently named here and throughout the country, but never examined or discussed, and, consequently, but imperfectly comprehended. The word has long served the demagogue for clap trap, and has furnished the alarmist with all his stock in trade. More, doubtless, is to be heard of it in the future; and as we of the Democratic party, who are unwilling to baptize the folly and corruption of the present Administration into wisdom and propriety, are charged with fostering and encouraging it, I may, perhaps, be tolerated for an hour in the statement of a few plain facts, which, strangely enough, in this connection, seem to have been overlooked or forgotten.

Sectionalism arises as well from the omission of acts as the commission of acts; in withholding from a portion of the people what they properly demand, as well as in aggression upon legal and well-defined rights. Our Government was intended by its founders to confer equal benefits, and to impose equal responsibilities; and whenever it shall fail in either of these objects, complaints will necessarily and justly arise. Then will it have lost that peculiar feature which gives to it all its winning charm and beauty, and there will be nothing left of it to be especially desired.

Sectionalism, as I understand it, is inequality and injustice, and can have no open defender. It ends where monarchy and absolutism begin, and therefore can never be tolerated or countenanced in a land of liberty. A tendency toward it is the surest sign of degeneracy and decay, and, when once established, the end of our republican experiment will be at hand. But if it lacks undisguised defence, it has its patrons in all those who are laboring for exclusive legislation, who would build up and fortify one portion of our country upon the ruins of another, and who would forget that our Government secures to us a common destiny.

There is a sectionalism in acts, if not in advocacy. The North have long suffered from it—in their commerce, their manufactures, their agriculture, their mechanic arts, their equality, and their inherent political rights and powers. We have long borne wrongs and forborne complaints; we have asked, and been denied; we have begged, and been spurned; we have struggled, and been overcome. Through our timidity, our subserviency, and our strifes, have we failed in our claims, our petitions, and our trials. We have solicited when our rights were plain; we have implored when we should have demanded; we have divided when we should have been united. For this we should not blame the South, but the North; and not so much the people of the North as the politicians of the North. We have been cursed by a breed of men who represented themselves, and not their constituencies; and at last, as was right, their selfishness was unrewarded, their ambition uncrowned, and their treachery rebuked. They have granted boons without returns; have compromised and lost all. If we have not been utterly sacrificed, it has not been because our leaders have not deserted us. If we have grown and prospered, it has been because of God's favor, and not of man's help.

Sir, if ninety Representatives in this Hall can control one hundred and forty-seven; if thirty Senators yonder can govern thirty-six; if fifteen feeble States can rule over eighteen powerful ones; if minorities can overcome majorities, and weakness strength, let us not further degrade ourselves by whining complaints against the former; but let us, in as manly a way as we may be able to do so, acknowledge their superiority over us, and have it written down in the archives of the nation, that our children may understand it, and learn their plain duty from it. If any one supposes I entertain a feeling of animosity towards my Southern brethren, let me here and now disabuse him. I commend them; I admire them for their boldness and success. But whilst I do so, I have an unspeakable contempt for that pusillanimity which enables them to exercise the one and to accomplish the other. I would have them imitated in their State pride and lack of gold-greediness; in their zeal, their energy, their frankness, and their skill. If we were more like them, we would suffer less, and they would respect us more. They would not then secure all the powers of Government, and all the patronage of office. Our Northern Presidents would be full-grown men; commanders-in-chief of the army and navy; executing the laws, suppressing incipient treason, and maintaining the spirit of our institutions. Our cringing Buchanans would be moulded into inflexible Jacksons, and the times of honesty and confidence, of quiet and good feeling, would be restored.

Instead of this order and harmony, which should characterize a common brotherhood, we have become discordant, and oftentimes almost belligerent. For the last ten years, at least, has this been the unhappy condition of our country. Sectionalism has been nursed and animated, until it has become the fruitful and commanding parent of all our national afflictions; not a sectionalism from the North, but from the South; not springing from the few who have been unable to learn the compromises of the Constitution and the value of our fathers' compact, but from the many who, feeling their weakness, have united for strength; a sectionalism not generated in the bracing air which cools the brow of the virtuous and intelligent laborer, but of the fetid and feverish atmosphere of rice swamps and cotton fields; not cultivated in green pastures, beside still waters, but upon plains burnt and blasted, as by hurricanes of fire; a sectionalism not of the farm and workshop, but of the lounge, the hammock, and the veranda. It is not plebeian, but a gentlemanly thing, that awes Presidents, fascinates lawgivers, and directs the ship of state. Now it is gentle and persuasive, then fierce and persistent, and at all times untiring and triumphant. It possesses no inherent force; our connivance alone arms it. It is the emblem upon the shield of Alcibiades: as the child it would be mild and harmless, but we give it the thunderbolt, and make it fearful and destructive.

The cause of our distraction and dissension is the agitation of questions connecting themselves with slavery; and I would impress this truth upon the public mind, that it is the determination to extend rather than reduce that institution which has arrayed the sections in apparent, if not actual, hostility. Each succeeding day but makes it the more evident that slavery expansion is the omnipresent and ruling consideration, alike in theology, in politics, and government. If I am mistaken, why do churches wrangle, and then sever? What has threatened periodically the stability of the Union? How will you account for the widespread alarm of 1850, and the misnamed compromises of that year? Why do our chief officers become intemperate partisans instead of temperate rulers? Whence arises the necessity for subverting party principles, changing party policy, and destroying party platforms? In what direction shall we look for that powerful agency which distinguishes between equals; in the one case conferring sovereignty, and in the other withholding it? Whose cupidity is ever reaching out frantically to seize the native African, and to clutch bordering domains; giving material aid and defence to the filibuster and land pirate; provoking proclamations of war from abroad, and inciting to bootless instructions for order at home? And to what cause shall we attribute the perpetual failure of all measures conducive to agricultural and mechanical growth and development?

Mr. Chairman, in the last half of the eighteenth century, when the republican patriots of France and America affirmed the freedom and equality of all men by birth and nature, our colonies accepted the declaration as an axiom, and rested upon it as the rock of their hope. Around it they kindled and fed the fires of the Revolution; and shivering and in rags upon the ice of winter, and fainting and wasted upon the sands of summer, they defended it with their lives, their fortunes, and their honor. They saved it and consecrated it. On it rests all our institutions. It is the great shrine which our fathers covered with their blessings, as the Cherubim covered with their wings the ark of the covenant of the Lord. Now it is assaulted so frequently, it neither excites interest nor occasions remark. A new gospel has been preached to the nation, and the man who values either his character or repose will be careful not to molest the modern orthodoxy by vain attempts to resuscitate the past. Those traitor zealots, who were so misguided as to give their labors to God and posterity, died too soon to learn the lie they had advocated, and how little they had achieved. It is well it was so, for they barely escaped the day when, if living, they would have been followed and taunted by derisive and detractive epithets; and when a Federal chief, sitting giddy-headed in the chair of Washington and Jefferson, would have opened upon them the vials of his indecent wrath, and demanded them in sacrifice, to appease the vengeance of those who must always despise him. Largely connected with the institution, they did not permit the consideration of slavery to interfere with the discharge of that plain duty they believed they owed the cause of mankind. Thinking it right to rebuke wrong, they did so in plain and unambiguous language. They were not theorists merely, but practicalists. They looked forward to an unconfined liberty, and declared absolute, perpetual bondage inimical to the education, opinions, social life, and every moral quality of those who were surrounded by it. We are not permitted to follow either their example or their precepts. Silence, even, will not leave us unmolested. We are now required, under the impending pains and penalties of party anathemas and proscription, to declare the enslavement of a weaker race to be patriarchal and heaven-ordained; and that those who fought our battles, and framed and shaped our Government, were banded infuriates and silly philanthropists. In this land, there are as yet no chains forged for the intellect, which may not be broken; and we will never allow either our faith or our confidence to be skackled. It was this exaction made of believing Christians, to array themselves against the sentiment of the world, and to proclaim slavery a sacred institution, which has divided the churches, and laid the foundation for that remarkable propagandism which professes to rely upon the Divine favor for its ultimate ascendency and success. The conquest of the Southern church to the sanction and interests of slavery has given it a city of refuge which it always before lacked, and has made it bold in the enormity of its demands. We are required to fall down and worship it. This is a sectional view that we never can sanction; and we appeal to the justice of God and the moral sense of men to sustain us in our refusal.

The effort to justify the origin of slavery, however it may be regarded by those taught in a different theology, cannot be more objectionable than the means used to coerce them into its adoption. Some of these it is my purpose to refer to; and I regret that I do not command the time to speak of them with that particularity which is demanded by their importance.

The people of the Northern States entertain a loyal attachment to the Constitution and the Union. Those who would deny the declaration have fallen into the mistake of assuming the singularities of a few to be a type of the mass. We will maintain the Federal compact in its integrity. There is no law, written, organic, or statute, against which we will raise the hand of rebellion; and we are fast forming the determination to restrain others from doing so. There is no record of a time when we fell short of a discharge of our whole duty. We have not only fought our own battles, but the battles of a common brotherhood. We have striven long because we loved well, and we gathered victory because we were devoted. We have branded treason, rebuked fanaticism, and kept the faith. And now, having thus acted, strategy makes use of our patriotism to overcome us. Those in the South for whose rights and welfare we have struggled and exhausted ourselves through long and arduous campaigns, feeling our passion for the Union to be our weakness, break in upon our needed rest, and startle our fears with its threatened dissolution. This cry always comes from the same quarter, and is sectional. It has been wonderful, magical in its office. It has secured tribute, subsidies, and esteem. Where our judgments would deny, our hearts have granted; and, stung by our wrongs, we have even caressed their cause. This cry that has so often startled the nation in the past, "*the Union is in danger*," has by no means been a groundless one. It has been in danger. It has been placed in surroundings of danger by the political speculator, for the mere purpose of having it saved. It will be again in danger; how frequently it may be so, it is not for me to predict; but this I will venture to declare, that danger will periodically assail it, until the lessons of justice shall be better learned on the one hand, or concessions shall be refused upon the other. Whenever that danger has existed, security, transient from its very nature, has been easily purchased, and always at the same price—by weakening the strength of one portion of the Union, and by strengthening the weakness of another portion of the Union. The consumptive system of slavery can no longer feed upon itself and live. It is to be nourished by milk drawn from the healthy breast of vigorous liberty. The sinking energies of the one are to be invigorated and sustained at the expense of the stalwart natural energies of the other. In this way, is an equilibrium to be maintained in the Republic. The laws of God and nature are to be counteracted, and principles of vastly unequal forces, and always at war with each other, are to be made coequal by human enactments. Shall God or man rule? Shall the temporal law repeal the eternal law? If the Union is to be preserved, it will be by bulwarks, and not by flight. Secession, now so flippantly promised, is a violation of more than sworn obligation; it is worse than treason; it is the destruction of the happiness of a numberless posterity; it earns the felon's death; and we trust its punishment first to him whom we shall call to preside over our destinies; and if he fails us, then to self-preservation and the unconquerable energies of truth, as it presides in the hearts of educated freemen.

The years from 1844 to 1850, inclusive, will long be remembered, from the most remarkable, as it was the most bold and adroit sectional movement known to our history. It had for its object a gigantic slavery extension, but under-a pretext very different in its form. It was nothing less than the forcible acquisition of one-half if not the whole of Mexico, for the purpose indicated, under color of the annexation of Texas. It is worse than folly to suppose that the determination to sustain what the South call the balance of power, but which would be more appropriately named the supremacy of power, has only just been determined upon. It has long been a settled policy with Southern leaders, recognising in it, as they do, the condition of the life of slavery. And how is the correctness of their view to be resisted? That man who has read the history of his race, and has not closed his eyes against the plain teaching of events transpiring daily around him, will never be convinced that there can be an enduring peace between slavery and freedom. Truces may be agreed upon, but they will be like the compacts of kings, made to be broken, whenever interest, ambition, passion, or progress, shall will it. Air lines may define rival States, but they never can bound conflicting sentiment. The vigorous and the true will invade the sickly and the false. The light of the press, the mechanical agencies and other productions of highly-cultivated art, the green fields and profuse harvests of scientific agriculture, the wide-spread wings of prosperous commerce, and the flooding wealth of ceaseless thrift, are not to be restricted by river banks, or corner stones, or parallels of latitude. These influences are forever and ever at work. They are your zealots, your fanatics, your traitors, your abolitionists, eternally preaching of the noblest triumphs of civilization, and impressing their lessons upon the hearts of the most inconsiderate and wayward. They are the invincible antagonists of ignorance, indolence, sterility, and poverty, and none but the unwise or disingenuous should attempt to deny it. When you can wall them in, you can control the travels of reason and the mightiest impulses of humanity. Then you may "bind the influences of Pleiades, and loose the bands of Orion." Then you may "bring forth Mazzaroth in his season," and "guide Arcturus with his sons."

It is not the handful of men planting sedition, and warring openly against legal institutions and fundamental law, which the States South fear, and against whose acts they seek protection through expansion. It is the reflection from the whole surface of the States North—their intelligence, skill, production, enterprise, and prosperity, which threaten and disturb. To foster and encourage these is to augment the danger. Not to attempt to counteract them would indicate an abandonment of the struggle—the breaking down of the Trajan bridge. I see here the cause of all the agitation upon the slavery question, in Congress and out of Congress, for the last fifteen years. Herein lies the secret of the contests for the Territories, the violation of covenants and compromises, and the appalling aggressions upon the sovereign rights of the people. The South seek the acquisition and tenure of the Territories; and what better agency, let me inquire, can they employ, to fortify themselves? Once surrounding us by a belt of States which should regard our institutions as inimical to theirs, we might well anticipate the fate of the Man in the Iron Shroud. With the powers of the General Government thus placed beyond our control, the walls would constantly contract upon us, until, at last, we should be crushed by the pressure; or, if left to survive, it would be upon some rugged mountain top, dwarfed to the insignificance of San Marino. Here I point to the cause and source of that sectional antagonism which must continue until either the North or the South shall gain the ascendency. Time will cast our country's horoscope; but let us still trust that it will remain her good fortune to exercise a humanizing and Christianizing sway over an injured and distorted humanity. There *is* such a thing as "manifest destiny;" and the destiny of the South is perfectly manifest to every one except themselves.

Sir, a few foot-prints in the past point out unmistakably the direction in which events have been hurrying us. The least noticed of these, at the time, was the daring resolve of party leaders to set aside the expressed and known will of the Democratic voters in the selection of a Chief Magistrate. As Mr. Van Buren was cast off in this way, and without damage to those engaged in the plot, it has never since been considered unsafe for a delegated body to engage in usurpation, or to give to their edicts the force of obligation. This is a great mischief, but by no means the most grievous result of the act; for upon it may be charged one of the greatest outrages, as I conceive, our people have ever been called upon to endure. I allude to the enactment of the compromise measures of 1850, and the fruits they have produced. By the great body of the then dominant party of the country, Mr. Van Buren had been virtually placed in nomination for the Presidency; but because he failed to see that necessity for the immediate annexation of Texas which was felt by others, delegates from Pennsylvania, even, who had given written pledges to sustain him, were among the earliest to sacrifice their plighted faith and the wishes of those they presumed to represent. The contrivance was successful, and the issue born. But, I am glad to know, the monster proceeded from no Northern womb; we did but act as midwives at the birth. The annexation achieved, as was foreseen by its parents, the war with Mexico, and an acquisition of her soil foreordained, as was supposed, for slavery, followed as closely-linked resulting consequences. But as God sometimes ventures to overrule the plottings of men, even the wisest of men, an unseen hand was at work to disappoint purposes, bringing good out of evil. As

Arlotta's bath in the brook, by attracting the attention of Duke Robert of Normandy, led to the establishment of the British empire, so a shovel-full of earth, carelessly thrown up near Suter's old fort, wrested California from blight and mildew, and converted it into Arcadian pastures and vine-wreathed vales. The discovery then made was the real philosopher's stone, which gave a golden throne to Freedom, and planted her victorious banners on the shores of the broad Pacific. So far, well; but now the folly and submission began. Those who had secretly played with stocked cards for the prize, and lost it, still made claim and showed their hands; and the winners, always magnanimous—rich in present gains—agreed to pay bounty for their daring and their enterprise. Yes, California, with area enough to make three States larger than New York, with a population more than sufficient to entitle her to two Representatives in this Hall, and with a Constitution desired by her people, was denied admission into the Union because of her choice of institutions, although purely republican in their form. Preferring the energy and productiveness of white labor to the sloth and sterility of black, we were required, I may say constrained, to buy her in as a sister, and at a price fixed by the usurer. As I am on the subject of sectionalism, it may be expected I should be particular as to the consideration yielded.

In the first place, we gave the fugitive slave law, and bound three million of adult freemen, engaged in professions, trades, and agriculture, to leave their books and tools and plows, to seek after and retake the running property of those who refused the captors the equality guarantied by the Constitution and the justice demanded by the spirit of the Government.

In the second place, having, by the resolutions of annexation, conceded to Texas, with a title to less than one hundred and seventy thousand square miles of territory, the astounding right to multiply her power—to divide and subdivide herself into at least five slave States, to be represented by at least ten Senators—we, in the flooding of grateful hearts, but with eyes blinded as by cataracts, made her a free gift of additional domain, sufficient in extent to constitute two States as large as Ohio, and bound the public Treasury to pay her ten million of dollars and interest, that she might the sooner avail herself of the monstrous prerogatives conferred upon her.

In the third place, although the father of "the compromise measures" declared that slavery did not exist, by law, in any of the territory acquired from Mexico, the demand was made, and agreed to, that it might be extended over Utah and New Mexico, comprising near half a million square miles of surface. In a word, these were the humiliating concessions made to the South as far back as 1850, not in return for acts of grace or good will, but seemingly as a propitiation for the enormity of having petitioned for a plain right. Such is the statesmanship of barratry and the statesmanship of bungle, over which praises have been sung to cover up disgrace.

The South have a settled policy; the North have none. The South have the policy of sectional interest and advantage; the North lack even that of consistent and persistent opposition. When they would make oblations to their peculiar institution, they clothe themselves in the mantle of a pretended patriotism, and declaim on the sacredness of the Constitution; but when we venture to ask a sustaining hand for ours, they would disfigure us by attempts to gird us with sackcloth, and filling our ears with the yelp and taunt of sectionalism. And I should like some one to name to me a President who, within the last decade at least, has not contemptuously turned his back upon those to whom he promised fairness, whose votes were necessary to his promotion, and who really constitute the right arm of the nation. Let him be named, if possible, for I confess I have never known him, even by repute. They have all—yes, all—been living commentaries upon the insecurity of platform professions and the spirit of submission, if not forgiveness, in the betrayed elector. The present Executive has not so much rendered himself notorious by his mere partiality, as he has by the disgusting subserviency displayed in his rule. His cajolery and deception as a candidate have only been excelled by his cynical demeanor to his true friends as an officer. He has valued phrases of flattery above the honest support of disinterested friendship, and prefers retirement, amid the execration of his neighbors, to the eulogies which wait upon faithful service. A self-relying and self-sustaining manhood would induce him to look above and beyond the artificial or painted horizon by which the trickster seeks to limit his vision, and not allow himself to be made a partisan and dupe. But when we find our confidence betrayed, and decency insulted, let us not blink the cause. Those communities which, harmonized by a common concern, take advantage of our want of unity and purpose, impress the placeman and spoilsman with the notion that they hold the keys of honor and of fortune. There is something here to study and to learn.

The South have necessities, and act upon them. The North have necessities, and sink into dreamy slumber. We fail to observe the steady steppings of the invader, but get into a frightful bustle when his guns begin to thunder at our city walls. The South are vociferous for party, as long as its machinery works unerringly to their advantage. The North are satisfied with declarations of a governmental policy, without regard to its success; and exult over platforms, whilst all their embodied principles are being violated. I cannot sanction the course pursued, either by the South or by the North. It is unfair; it is unjust. That of the South is sectional and aggressive; that of the North, yielding and self-destructive. Deprecating anarchy and war, I desire, above all things, an honest maintenance of the compact between these United States, in its integrity. Sustaining Democracy, I protest against its being made a catch and a cheat. Born and living in one of the most powerful, prosperous, intelligent, and generous of the free States, I will not admit a right of superiority over our citizens, either by nature, education, or grace.

In 1856, there was nothing better understood than the doctrines and pledges of the National Democracy. They were plainly written, and received but one interpretation. Popular sovereignty *over all domestic institutions* was declared to be as perfect and complete in the resident of a Territory as in the citizen of a State; and that party bound itself to its faithful maintenance. If it was sound and undeniable before the election, it was not the less so afterwards. But no; it failed in practice. It failed to accomplish what it was believed by many it would accomp'ish, and therefore it was repudiated. It failed to give Kansas to slavery. It failed to make eight million of men, without industrial habits and colonizing capacity, superior to eighteen million with these auxiliaries, in their race for new sovereignties; and thenceforward it was enrolled in the catalogue of humbugs. It failed to aid the sectional purposes of the South, and thenceforward to favor it became heterodox; and all who have done so, from that day to this, have been branded with treason, and trodden down beneath the iron heel of a fear-struck, renegade President. The end ought to have been seen from the beginning. On the 19th of March, 1856, when this doctrine was at the flood-tide of its popularity, I ventured to use this language here:

"Sir, the supporters of that bill [the Kansas-'Nebraska bill] have proclaimed to the nation 'that the Territories of the United States are 'to constitute 'a fair field,' and that there is to 'be a 'free fight' there, between the North and 'the South, to decide whether slavery or freedom shall rule them. If the energy, the enterprise, the active modes of life, the available 'capital, and the numbers, of the North, shall 'not be able to compete successfully with their 'opposites in the South, and secure freedom 'to the Territories, then I will admit that there 'is a vitality and a power in slavery which we 'of the North have never dreamed of. In my 'opinion, the Representatives of the South 'in the Thirty-third Congress 'have sown the 'fire, and they will gather fire into their own 'garners.'"

I have only to add, that the correctness of my views has been proven at an earlier day than I then anticipated, and that the pang of repentance now comes too late. The choice to be made by the South—and I admit it is for them a severe one—is between the rigid observance of existing law, which will shut out slavery from the Territories by a popular vote, and Congressional intervention directly to exclude it. The next census, if fairly taken, will show such a preponderance of population on the side of the North as to convince the most skeptical on this point.

But there are more appalling evidences of the sectionalism I charge. These are found in acts of glaring lawlessness and disorder, and in the determination to cripple and impoverish Northern labor.

Sir, there are eighteen States of this Union, and soon there will be twenty-three, extending from the Atlantic to the Pacific, and across fifty-eight degrees of longitude, teeming with millions of men, controlling and directing the literature, commerce, agriculture, manufactures, and mechanic arts, of the whole country; fruitful in peace, and able for war, who will not soon forget the early history of Kansas, and the suffering of their friends and kinsmen there, through violence and fraud. It was there the lesson was industriously taught and fully learned, that the rightful rule of the people over all their institutions meant but the sanction and acceptance of slavery; and that a President of the United States could be as false as other men. It was there the people ascertained, for the first time, that the power to form and regulate institutions, conferred upon them by their organic act, and which Mr. Buchanan informed them had an especial reference to slavery, would confer sovereignty, or deny it, just as its exercise might be congenial or uncongenial to slavery; that the people of a Territory were under a constitutional obligation to legislate for its benefit, but could under no circumstances legislate against it; that a Territory was virtually a slave State; that popular sovereignty, which before an election was admitted to be alike in State and Territory, was a naked right and obligation to assist the South against the North in a contest between them, which was to end in the superiority of the one and the inferiority of the other; and that when a majority, deceived by artifice, would not consummate the dishonesty, it should be perfected by ruffian invasion, stuffed ballot-boxes, and the bayonets of the Federal army. These States will not be likely to overlook all this. When they shall do so, their future will be made up, and might as well be written out.

Unfortunately, it is not permitted us longer to doubt the existence of Southern sectional schemes, and of the inefficiency alike of laws, treaties, and proprieties, to restrain them. In the infancy and innocency of the Republic, the inhumanity, criminality, and impolicy of the slave trade were admitted, and denounced under severe penalties; now, however, intelligence, character, influence, and wealth, are directed in its favor. Although the Constitution looked to its suppression after the year

1808, the statutes made in pursuance thereof are treated as unconstitutional, without any adjudication against them, and rewards offered to the depraved and venal, to treat them as nullities. How this conduct may appear to others, I cannot say; but to my mind it looks to the destruction of Government, and comes with an exceedingly ill grace from a quarter appealing to a few in the North, equally extreme in their notions, to love and abide by the law. Federal courts fail to punish the offenders; and he who all his life has breathed the air of freedom, and sworn to execute the laws, gives to them the strongest manifestations of his approbation and esteem. This movement, carrying with it, as it does, the plainest admission that the South require additional labor to cultivate their lands; indeed, that their necessities in this respect are so overruling as to constrain them forcibly to subvert the very foundations of all safe government, does not restrain them from the significant absurdity of demanding for their slaves not merely the territory already belonging to the nation, but even Cuba, Central America, and Mexico. If the South have any reason for aiding, encouraging, and shielding, the filibuster, which they are willing to declare, it is found, unquestionably, in this pretence. This is, then, their position, and to the maintenance of which, as I infer, they mean, sooner or later, to commit the Democratic party, and to have recognised by Congressional action. It may be thus plainly stated: slaves are now so high in price, and lands so low, as to show a great demand for the former; and therefore the foreign slave trade must be renewed, and the laws abolishing it repealed. Then, again, slave territory must be added, to afford an outlet for surplus labor; and, to acquire it, treaties must be broken down, the national honor tarnished, and the country, if needs be, embroiled in servile, civil, and foreign wars. Here, I presume, we are to look for that true conservative nationalism which, under the patronizing guidance of Presidents, Cabinets, and small officials, brands Northern devotion to the Union, the Constitution, the laws, and the sound principles of republican government, as sectional and unfriendly. Such demands must be resisted to the last. They can mean but one thing; and, unchecked, they can end in but one thing—unlimited slavery expansion, and the subjection of the North.

Southern statesmen and politicians, resting upon the conclusion, to force slavery into the mastery over freedom, the North is not only to be shackled, but weakened by starvation. Directing all their efforts to erect a line of slave battlements around the free States, we could scarcely expect them to strengthen our means of resistance, and consequently we must not be surprised to find all kindly and genial legislation denied us. Those who see nothing significant in the failure here, or in the Senate, of all measures conducive to the interests of Northern capital and labor, are invariably the least reflective of our people, and those who are most safely relied upon to make up party Conventions, and so to shape their faces as to receive a master's smile. The North ask but a fair share of the benefits of Government, and they will soon have it, in the only way by which it should be reached: by doing equal and exact justice, and by forcing others to follow their example. It is possible, I know, that, mortified by defeat, those who drive us to this resolve may desire to follow the example of Sardanapalus, to fire the temple and perish in the flames; but we will save both it and them.

Sir, this discussion has been to me by no means a pleasant one; but the general charge of fanaticism so constantly thundered against the North, because of mere individual delinquencies, has become so nauseating, that I have felt myself forced into it. I have stated my facts and drawn my conclusions. They are true and legitimate, and I throw them before the country, desiring but an impartial judgment upon them. I criminate the accusers, and prove them guilty of the charge they themselves prefer. The South are the accusers, and sectionalism their accusation; and how can they explain away the circumstances I have arrayed against them—requiring the church to justify slavery; driving the North into an acquiescence in their demands, that the Union may be shielded; closing the doors against free States, until the capricious price fixed for their admission is paid; proselyting Presidents to Southern schemes; using the enunciations of party for local and selfish purposes, by allowing or denying sovereignty to the people, as their interests may incline; disregarding the most sacred compacts and statutes, in reopening the slave trade and encouraging land piracy to build up slave States; and withholding all legislation favoring the growth and prosperity of the North? Certain it is, if the North ever entered the lists for sectional profit, they have been far outstripped in the race.

Mr. Chairman, you value highly your title to American citizenship, because it is honorable. It has been made so by the natural operations of the political system under which we live. Our Constitution was framed in liberality and justice; and until recently we have all reverenced it. Its humane principles, rather than soil and climate, have made us a great nation. It recognises no birthright prerogatives, and disposes, as far as possible, of all artificial distinctions between men. It records no single selfish thought; on the contrary, its philanthropy is as broad as the earth. It has made our country a father to the fatherless, a refuge for the pursued and persecuted—the citadel of freedom. It has doubled our population, peopled new States, increased productive enterprise, vindicated its origin, and established the sacred character of its mission. As far as human forecast can discover, the only obstacle in the broad road of empire which Providence seems to have marked out for us, is the conflict of sectional institutions and interests. If this cannot be prevented, it certainly need not be encouraged. I have no right, directly or indirectly, to interfere with the domestic establishments of my friend in South Carolina, and I deny his right to interfere with mine. We are both shielded by the same law. If mine have merits to recommend them above his, and powers and influence beyond his, that is his ill fortune or his ill choice, and he must not quarrel with me on that account, much less contend that his shall be accepted. Early Christianity disturbed the business of Demetrius, lessening the demand for silver shrines; but he was not justified on that account for insisting upon the worship of Diana. Each must be left to the people, for their unrestricted acceptance or rejection, as advantage, convenience, or fancy, may dictate. They will eventually dispose of all such difficulties, whether we will it or not.

It is popular power, sir, that has made us what we are; it will lead us on to a dazzling future. In the mean time, men will have nightmares, and awake to blissful realities; prophecies of disaster will be made and falsified; faith will fail and be restored; embarrassments will be interposed and brushed away. Even now, no ocean strand limits the force of our example. We have a written history without a parallel in the annals of our race. We have touched the disguises of tyranny as with the spear of Ithuriel. After six thousand years of unavailing effort, it was reserved for us to truthfully map and define the political attributes of man. In three-quarters of a century we have advanced from a few feeble colonies to numerous and mighty States. From the wilderness we have carved out the fruitful field, cultivated the products of all soils and climates, and fed starving millions. We have built more cities than Thebes had gates; invented steamboats and telegraphs; made railroads; opened mines; and, by the aid of the mechanical genius of our people, are on the eve of supplying the world with the fruits of our arts. We now stand in the front rank of earthly Powers—not as a nation of warriors, born to the work of death, but as a nation of men educated to the trades of life; not degenerated and loaded with chains, but in perfect stature and unfettered will. Shall all this be sacrificed to the weakness of the foolish, the aspirations of the selfish, or the machinations of the wicked? The public heart responds quickly to mine, "Never! no, never!" and there is safety.

WHO HAVE VIOLATED COMPROMISES.

SPEECH

OF

HON. JOHN HICKMAN,

OF PENNSYLVANIA.

Delivered in the House of Representatives, December 12, 1859.

WASHINGTON, D. C.
BUELL & BLANCHARD, PRINTERS.
Stereotyped by Blanchard's Patent, issued February 22, 1859.
1859.

Speech of Mr. Hickman.

The *Constitution* newspaper, the organ of Mr. Buchanan's Administration, having charged upon the Anti-Lecompton Democracy a bargain with the Republicans to effect an organization of the House—

Mr. HICKMAN said:

Mr. Clerk, with regard to the attack made by the President's newspaper on myself and others, I have but a word to say. If made by the President himself, he knows it to be false. If made by any other person, he does not know it to be true; for, sir, the reason why I occupy the position here to-day which I do occupy, is because I could not be purchased. [Applause from the Republican benches and from the galleries.] This reading me out of the Democratic party has been faithfully persevered in for the last four years, by many abler and stronger than the gentleman from Missouri, [Mr. NOELL,] and still they have not yet got rid of me, and it will take them perhaps four years longer of persevering effort, if I shall choose to remain so long in their good company.

My "treason," to which very frequent reference has been made here, not merely during the present session, but during former ones, has a history connected with it—a history with which the gentleman from Missouri ought to be acquainted. Sir, it dates back four years, when, in this Hall, on the grievous charge being made—a charge which pervaded the country, and which was believed by the country—that fraud and force and all manner of crimes had so far invaded the Territory of Kansas that they had prostrated thoroughly the people, I chose to introduce a resolution to investigate that charge. That was the time when my treason commenced, for I then took the stand against an undivided Democracy; and, sir, I charge on that undivided Democracy, from whom I do dissent to-day—not, however, because I have failed to be a Democrat—a persevering effort, both in this Hall and in the other wing of the Capitol, to stifle that investigation and to suppress the proof of the fraud. Then, sir, I was read from the Democratic party; and yet, after the committee, which I was, to some extent, instrumental in raising, (and this is the first time I have ever referred to it,) had made their report to Congress, no man in the country was sufficiently reckless to deny that the charge which had been preferred was fully and completely proved. Then, sir, I was denounced as a renegade and a traitor, and for what? What was the body of my offence? Because I chose to differ from the Democracy, believing that the charge ought to be investigated, and that, if fraud existed, it ought to be revealed. And have they ever washed their hands of it to this day? No, sir; to no greater extent than silence may have done it.

Well, sir, I returned home to my people with all the brand of treason which that body of men could place upon my forehead; and Mr. Buchanan, the present President of the United States, endorsed my Democracy in the face of that accusation which had gone up against me, and insisted on my renomination, as he believed that it would be valuable to his canvass. Mr. Buchanan did not denounce me.

Now, a word in respect to that canvass, for the mere purpose of instituting a brief inquiry as to where the charge of "treason" may properly rest, and as to who is the renegade. The State of Pennsylvania was in very imminent peril at that election; and Mr. Buchanan knew that the election in that State rested upon the answer to a single inquiry, which was this: Was it safe to trust him with the management of Kansas affairs? Why, sir, it can be proved by a thousand living witnesses, if necessary, that during that summer, this man, who now fills the Executive chair, made it his business to pledge men, everywhere in the North, that if he should succeed in his election, as he knew the Free-State element in that Territory to be the stronger, Kansas should come into the Union as a free and not as a slave State. That fact has been frequently stated. It has never been denied in Pennsylvania; and by means of the pledges that he thus gave, did he succeed in carrying that State at the November election. As soon, however, as he reached the city of Washington, it was discovered that the mind of the President had undergone a very sudden change—not that his judgment was convinced, because I think it can be very clearly shown that he never alleged that his mind had undergone any change up to that time; but he made the fear that three or four Southern States would secede from the Union a pretext for urging upon Congress the adoption of the fraudulent Lecompton Constitution. Then, we begged leave to differ from him in his policy. We were again denounced as traitors, and again read out of the Democratic party. Well, sir, the President's hand was raised against us, and everything that Executive power and patronage could do was done for the purpose of destroying us in our respective districts. We are now back here again, to rebuke again the treachery of this wicked and reckless and leprous Administration; and if that is treason, the other side have got to make the most of it.

I have said all that I propose to say upon that point at this time. I may avail myself of another opportunity to go into it at greater length.

Well, sir, the charge of treason that has been made is not sufficiently powerful to humiliate and disgrace us, and we find this newspaper adding to it an allegation of corruption. If there is any man in this body of men who knows of any contract or agreement that I have entered into with anybody, for any purpose, let him proclaim it now, or forever hereafter hold his peace. I have never done so anywhere, at any time; and I say now, that if the election of my friend, Col. Forney—and I take great pleasure in calling him my friend—could only be effected by such an arrangement—that if I could only procure his election as Clerk of this House by entering into a covenant with any man here, upon the Republican side of the House—I would refuse to do it. As Mr. Buchanan could not purchase me, so can I not be purchased by others. [Applause and hisses.] I have already been offered more than I am worth, and I refused to sell myself at that. [Laughter and applause.] Why, sir, this is all false pretence. I know where the trouble is, and the country knows where it is. I have ventured to express opinions against giving to Slavery an unlimited charter to travel where it pleases. That is the body of my offence; all the rest is false pretence. And I desire to say now, that if Democracy consists in supporting all the claims which the Southern country may make upon us, I shall very soon cease to be a Democrat. I have been in this House long enough to learn many things which I never could have learned at home, and I think it has perfected my education upon one point: I have learned that a man may support every measure of a Democratic Administration, and yet, if he shall vote against a single interest of Slavery, he ceases *ipso facto* to be a Democrat; but if he vote against every measure of the Administration, and will sustain the interests of Slavery, he is *ipso facto* a good Democrat. I put that as God's naked truth before this House and before the country, and I intend to stand upon it as a solemn conviction.

Now, sir, I wish to say a word to the Administration side of the House; and I intend, in what I say upon this occasion, and upon every other, to treat every man here as I would be treated myself, respectfully; but I shall express my opinions, if I choose to do so, all of them, fearlessly. There *is* a contest between the North and the South, and the admission might just as well be made now as at any future time. There *is* a state of feeling existing between the North and the South which cannot be removed; it is as deep laid as the foundations of mountains, and, sir, it pervades every section like an atmosphere. If you want to know why the North have feelings upon this subject, I will tell you. They have become satisfied that there is but one thing which will satisfy our Southern brethren; and that is, the right to carry Slavery everywhere, to plant it everywhere, to sustain it everywhere, against the united wishes, as it is against the united interests, of the North.

Mr. MOORE, of Alabama. Will the gentleman permit me to ask him a question?

Mr. HICKMAN. I interrupt nobody, and I do not wish to be interrupted myself, for I do not want to get into a controversy.

This determination to extend Slavery is Southern interest, and the Representatives of the South are compelled to ask as much. I do not complain of them for so doing; but when *our* interests are directly adverse to theirs, and lie in another direction, why should we be denounced for pursuing our interests as they pursue theirs?

More than this. The North has grievous charges to prefer against the South, and they are charges which they will have answered. That is my conviction; and if the expression of these sentiments stamps me with the title of Abolitionist, so be it; I will wear it as well as I can. Yes, sir, they have charges to make against the South, which they will have answered. They charge them with the violation of covenants, compacts, and compromises. That is what they charge them with, and it is well that they should know it. It is useless to cry peace, sir, when there is no peace. Why, sir, when the compromises of the Constitution were entered into by our fathers, it has been said that, if the same spirit had existed which exists now, those compromises never could have been made. I see the truth of the remark; I feel the truth of the remark, sir; for when those compromises were entered into, they were entered into under the solemn conviction that the power of Slavery from that day was not to increase, but to be diminished. If they had had the feelings or if they had pursued the policy which our Southern friends are now intent upon, those compromises never could have been entered into. What did they get? What did our Southern friends get by those compromises? They got the Slavery representation. They got the foundation for a fugitive slave law. They got exemption from export duties. They got three very large advantages. What did the North get, or what did the interests of Freedom get? Why, sir, they got the implied pledge, that, after the year 1808, the importation of Africans, or the foreign slave trade, should cease.

Now, sir, the South boast to-day that they are in full possession of all the benefits of all the compromises of the Constitution; that they have the Slavery representation; and, if I understood a gentleman who spoke a few days ago, he declared that they have here, by force of the three-fifths representation, twenty members upon this floor. They boast, sir, that they have the fugitive slave law, and that the North does not abide by its provisions. They are certainly exempt from duty upon exports; and where is the North, with her share of the compromises of the Constitution? Why, sir, we hear it boldly avowed, not here, but it will come here before spring, it will come before the flowers come, that they do not intend that the foreign slave trade shall be closed. They intend to open the traffic. Yes, sir, they have opened the traffic; they make bold to say so, and Southern courts refuse to punish offenders. I say, then, the North charges upon the South that they have swept away from the North the benefits of the compromises of the Constitution, when the South are in the full enjoyment of all the advantages which could possibly result to them.

When you come to the compromise of 1820; when, in order to get Missouri into the Union as a slave State, they gave to us of the North the solemn pledge and entered into bonds that Slavery should never exist north of the southern line of that State; after having got Missouri in, and reaped all the advantage which they could reap from that compromise, the South came here—not the North—the South came here, almost a united South, to say that the benefit which the North received from the compromise of 1820 should be swept away; and, sir, Southern breath swept it away; and we had, in consequence, the struggle in Kansas as to whether Slavery should or should not go into territory from which it had been prohibited.

But, sir, the North charge, further, that in the compromise of 1832—the great compromise of the great compromiser—Northern trade was paralyzed, and Northern industry destroyed. And then, sir, last, and not by any means least, we have the compromises of 1850 and 1854, which I choose to join together, as they constitute but one single compact. After we bought—yes, sir, after we bought California into the Union, giving to the South monstrous prerogatives, which I will not undertake now to enumerate, they made us the solemn guaranty that if we would adopt the principle of the Kansas-Nebraska bill, to leave the whole question of Slavery to the final determination of the people of the Territory, and exclude all agitation of the Slavery question from Congress, they would abide by it. Now, sir, where are we? Who is there that represents that Southern sentiment of 1850 and 1854, upon this floor? Who is there that represents it? Is there any Southern member who represents it? It is likely that there is. If there be, however, he has maintained a most respectful silence up to this moment. No, sir; the Southern sentiment destroys all the benefits which the North were to reap from the compromise of 1850 and 1854. I will not undertake to say what the motive of the gentleman was who introduced the Kansas-Nebraska bill, but I think that no man ought to have doubted what the effect of that bill would be. The South undoubtedly expected that it would conduce to the interest of Slavery, and the effort was strenuously made, I think, in Kansas, to force that benefit from the main provision of the bill. But from the moment that it failed to plant Slavery in Kansas, it has been repudiated; and if I understand the position which the South occupy to-day, it is that they will have nothing to do with this thing of squatter sovereignty. They bitterly despise and denounce it.

Now, here is the first, the second, the third, the fourth, and the fifth compromise which the North has entered into with the South upon this all-absorbing subject of Slavery; and the North charge upon the South, that, in every single instance of compromise, they have violated its sanctity, after having received the benefit, or tried to receive the benefit, arising from their side of the bargain. And these charges have to be answered—not here, merely, but at other times and other places. They will have to be answered next year, and I assume now the position that the South have got to satisfactorily explain these things, or they have got to give up the Federal offices. [Applause and cries of "Good" upon the Republican side.] Now, the South have rights, guarantied under the Constitution; but the South have not all the rights. The North have a few. Individually, I would not withhold from the South, or from any portion of the South, the least, as I would not the greatest right, guarantied to her either by fundamental law or statute. I would treat her as I would treat a younger sister; I would give her more than she is entitled to, rather than less, because she is the weaker party. I would bestow bounties, even, upon her; but when she comes here, or anywhere else, and demands, as a right, what is not her right, and seeks to wrest from the North what she is not entitled to, I would deny her. That is my position, and those are my principles at the present time; for if I understand the politics of the country, if I have not been blinded for the last four years, there are no politics in the United States now but "nigger." The whole politics of the country are involved in the negro question. Shall Slavery travel into the Territories, or shall it not? that is the question. There is no other question, and there will be no other question in the Presidential contest of 1860; and if I am constrained to choose between the party which insists that Slavery shall travel everywhere, against right, and that party which says it shall not go anywhere, even when it has a right, I cannot help it. That is all. I stand upon the principle of the Kansas-Nebraska bill. I believe it is sufficient for us. It is anyhow the bond between the North and the South, and I will try it a little further, and I am with the men who are for that principle. I know how it will result. It will result exactly where the Republicans desire it should end; it will end in the exclusion of Slavery from all the Territories of the United States. If there is any man who is committed to the principles of the Kansas-Nebraska bill, who does not answer that question in that way when it is propounded to him, all I have to say is, that he is either wilfully blind or slightly dishonest.

Sir, I have never uttered a political sentiment in my life, that I can remember, that I would not utter here, in the hearing of the South—not one. I have always stood by the Democratic party, when I believed it to be right. I adhere to the principles of the Democratic party; and I have always opposed that party when I believed it to be wrong, and I intend to do so forever. There shall not be any misunderstanding between any gentlemen upon the Democratic side of the House and myself. I feel perfectly certain that the party has been bankrupted by this Administration of James Buchanan. I know it. I know it; for whenever the Democratic party can no longer control Northern masses, then that party is bankrupt; and that is the condition of that party to-day. There is not a Northern State, not one, as there is scarcely a Northern county, that can be carried upon the doctrine upon which Mr. Buchanan this day bases his Administration. I want the party to put itself exactly right at Charleston; and, if it will not put itself right, I want it to put itself plainly wrong. I do not want the people, either of the North or of the South, to be deceived by any platform which can be interpreted in one way in one section and in another way in another section. If it is the sentiment of the Democratic party that Slavery shall travel with the column of our advancing civilization, I say, put it so before the people, express it plainly, and receive the Northern verdict upon it.

I should have said something about Union meetings at the North, but my friend from New York [Mr. HASKIN] has rendered that entirely unnecessary. I say this, which will cover everything I should have said at greater length: that there is no sentiment now in the North which can plant itself upon Southern policy, as I understand it, and live; for the reason that it would be governed by selfish considerations. And if this condition of things existing between the North and South shall lead to a dissolution of this Union, which no one would deplore more than I should; all I can say is, the North, under those circumstances, will endeavor to take care of themselves. I have never seen a Northern man, in latter times, that was much scared. I know many men have been alarmed, in times past, at the cries of dissolution; but I have never yet seen a Northern man who expressed any alarm as to the results of a dissolution of the Union. I will state what my conviction is on the subject. I do not know, however, that I thoroughly understand what is meant by a dissolution of the Union. If it means a dividing line of sentiment between the North and South, and virtual non-intercourse, why we have reached that dissolution already; for Northern men cannot now travel in the South; and, as I understand it, any postmaster in any village of the South, where the receipts of the office would not amount to five dollars, can, if a letter bearing my frank goes into his hands, open it, examine it, and burn it, on the pretext that it is incendiary. Sir, we have reached that dividing line between the North and the South. But, if dissolution means that there is to be a division of territory, by Mason and Dixon's line, or by any other line, I say "no;" that will never be. I express my opinion—and that opinion may go before the country, whether false or true—when I say "no;" the North will never tolerate a division of the territory. [Applause from the Republican benches.]

Mr. GARTRELL. I should like to know how you are to prevent it.

Mr. HICKMAN. I will tell you how it will be prevented. I am neither a prophet, nor the son of a prophet; but I express my belief that there is as much true courage in the North, though it may not be known by the name of chivalry, [sensation,] as there is in the South. I do not use the word contemptuously, for I admire true chivalry everywhere. There is as much true courage at the North as there is at the South. I always believed it, and, therefore, I will express it; and I believe, sir, that with all the appliances of art to assist, eighteen millions of men reared to industry, with habits of the right kind, will always be able to cope successfully, if it need be, with eight millions of men without these auxiliaries. [Great sensation, some applause from the Republican benches and the galleries, and hisses in other parts of the Hall.]

Mr. LEAKE. Will the gentleman permit me to propound to him a respectful interrogatory?

Mr. HICKMAN. I am up now, answering an interrogatory. I am answering why I am not a rascal. [Laughter and applause.] That is the main interrogatory.

I am sorry, sir, to trouble the House with these remarks. I entered this Hall on Monday with the firm determination that I would not be dragged into a speech. I found that it was impossible to maintain that determination, that attacks were to be made incessantly, continuously; attacks, too, that could not be passed over in silence. I have answered them. There is no charge resting upon me of corruption, either here or at home. If there had been any there, it would have been exposed long before this. I have passed between raking fires there, as I have here. My colleague [Mr. FLORENCE] smiles, for he knows something about it. If the charge could have been made, it would have been made and proven; and, therefore, I do not want any charge to be made against me here by any gentleman on this floor, much less by a contemptible, hoodwinked newspaper, at the other end of the avenue, which has not as much circulation as a decent Northern village journal, when they have discovered nothing to found a charge upon.

www.ingramcontent.com/pod-product-compliance
Lightning Source LLC
LaVergne TN
LVHW020742120826
845150LV00010B/2347
* 9 7 8 1 4 1 8 1 9 3 8 8 1 *